Note
by note

A Celebration of
the Piano Lesson

Tricia Tunstall

SIMON & SCHUSTER
New York   London   Toronto   Sydney

SIMON & SCHUSTER
1230 Avenue of the Americas
New York, NY 10020

Copyright © 2008 by Tricia Tunstall

First Simon & Schuster hardcover edition April 2008

SIMON & SCHUSTER and colophon are registered trademarks of Simon & Schuster, Inc.

For information about special discounts for bulk purchases, please contact Simon & Schuster Special Sales at 1-800-456-6798 or business@simonandschuster.com.

Book Design by Jaime Putorti
Illustrations by Irene Kelly

Manufactured in the United States of America

10   9   8   7   6   5   4   3   2   1

Library of Congress Cataloging-in-Publication Data

Tunstall, Tricia.
   Note by note : a celebration of the piano lesson / Tricia Tunstall.
      p. cm.
1. Piano—Instruction and study. I. Title.
MT220.T93 2008
786.2'193071—dc22   2007028303

ISBN-13: 978-1-4165-4050-2
ISBN-10:   1-4165-4050-4

For Adam and Evan

CONTENTS

CHAPTER ONE

Beginnings

*J*enny sits on my piano bench. Her feet swing freely; they will not reach the floor, not to mention the pedals, for another year or two. She stares at a note on the page of music in her open lesson book, her eyes wide, her tongue caught between her lips. "A," she whispers to herself. The seconds file slowly by, and then at last the third finger of her left hand presses a key. A furtive glance at me; was it right? I nod. She nearly smiles, and then her eyes return to the page. More seconds, loud with silence. "G," she murmurs.

For a six-year-old a piano lesson can be an act of courage. Every note is an occasion for worry, a tiny drama involving risk and consequence. Fingers perch awkwardly on the keys, so likely to be the wrong keys, or the wrong fingers. The black circles of the notes caught in the implacable grid of lines on the page are so easily mistaken for other notes tangled between other lines. There are numbers that mean fingers and there are numbers that mean beats; it is hard to know which is which. Sometimes I have to remind Jenny to breathe.

Do you remember your piano lessons? Most people do. There tends to be a visceral immediacy to these memories, a sensory sting. "Caramels," says my friend Eileen, "my teacher ate caramels while I played. She weighed three hundred pounds. I never got to eat a caramel." My sister-in-law Suzanne remembers the bumpy brick floor of the sitting room where she waited for her lesson, and the way the stained-glass windows in the piano studio cast a tawny light on her music. My teenage son Evan has a vivid image of the Ssips juice boxes at the house of his piano teacher (who was, needless to say, not me); as a six-year-old, he was deeply impressed both by the wondrous spelling of the word on the boxes and by the fact that he was not offered one. Long after one has forgotten how to play the Minuet in G, the memory remains of the piano teacher's perfume or garlic breath, the tassels on her lampshade, the sharp bark of her dog.

The piano teacher . . . or the flute teacher, or the violin teacher. In the course of a modern American childhood, there are very few occasions when a child spends an extended period alone with an unrelated adult. Classroom learning, athletic coaching, Sunday school—all these forms of instruction are group activities. But the music lesson is one on one. It requires a weekly session alone together, physically proximate, concentrating on the transfer of a skill that is complicated and difficult, often frustrating and frequently tedious, but that every now and then opens suddenly and without warning into joy.

In recent years there have been attempts, of course, to replace this arcane ritual with truly modern forms of instruction. There are instructional videos, printed manuals, on-line courses, all purporting to teach one to play the piano in twelve short months or ten easy steps. Ask any piano teacher: we are not worried. Our phones ring regularly with potential new students. We know that, mostly, people do not want "interactive programming" or "user-friendly software." People want piano lessons.

Even now, in a time when very little current popular music involves an actual person playing an actual piano—even now, parents want their children to have piano lessons. Adults wish their parents had given them piano lessons. Perhaps most surprising, children want piano lessons. There lingers in the culture a sense, however unexamined or anachronistic, that a truly complete education must include lessons in playing a musical instrument—the violin or flute or trumpet, sometimes, but most frequently, because it is the most accessible, the piano.

What is the enduring appeal of the piano lesson as a basic ritual of American childhood? I have spent a great deal of my life as a piano student, pianist or piano teacher, and I can only begin to guess at the reasons. What I can say—what I do know—is that piano lessons are not only about music but also about trust and confidence, chaos and order, spontaneity and discipline and patience, sometimes even about love . . . and once again, and always, about music: its beauty, its power, its capacity to convey profound emotions beyond the reach of words.

This is true from the beginning, the very earliest lessons. Jenny on my piano bench is not only learning where G is, she is learning to take risks. She is learning to trust me and, eventually, herself. And she is experiencing beauty, because when G follows A just exactly as it should, in the context of an emerging melody—well, it may not be profound, but it can be beautiful.

My first piano teacher was Dorothea Ortmann, daughter of the director of the Peabody Conservatory. When I was six she was terribly old, maybe even fifty. Her row house on Saint Paul Street in downtown Baltimore had three stories, and I sometimes thought I could hear pianos being played on all three floors simultaneously. I did not know who else was playing, but I decided that she had six grand pianos, two on each floor. Six would not have been too many for Miss Ortmann, whose life was clearly dedicated to the art of pianism in the grand European tradition. I would not have been surprised to learn that when her students had gone and she was left in dark brocaded solitude, she drifted up and down the stairs playing all the pianos, all night long.

Miss Ortmann had a dimly lit sitting room where on a side table sat a number of those once-popular miniature toy animals constructed of tiny segments of hollow wood through which a kind of rubber band was threaded; the animal stood upright until you pressed a circular disc beneath its base, when it would collapse. If you pressed the base gently and just on one side, you could make the animal bend its front or back legs, or even nod its head. I took these toys as evidence that the firm and methodical Miss Ortmann had a fun-loving side. Now, it occurs to me that she was encouraging finger dexterity in her waiting students.

I never did see her fun-loving side. She was gracious, she was cheerful, but she was very strict; I was transfixed and intimidated. Now, as I sit next to Jenny watching her spindly fingers, her fragile profile, it occurs to me that I was as acutely exposed to Miss Ortmann as Jenny is to me, and that her strict demeanor may have been her way of distancing herself from my vulnerability.

While in Jenny's eyes I am certainly very old, I am not Miss Ortmann, not as serious and formal. For one thing, I am chattier. In every first lesson, for example, I ask my new student what music he or she listens to. I don't believe it would have occurred to Miss Ortmann to ask such a question, although I would have loved to tell her about my little record player decorated with nursery rhyme characters. It played only forty-fives, and if there was dust on the needle—there was usually dust on the needle—the music would sound like something coming over a transistor radio at sea. My parents had given me a thick red leather volume of bound record sleeves filled with recordings of great classics, with the odd and wonderful result that to this day, Little Miss Muffet reminds me of Rachmaninoff's Second Piano Concerto, Red Riding Hood of Beethoven's Seventh Symphony. As for the recording quality, the first time I heard a symphony played live in a concert hall, I think I vaguely missed the static.

Had she asked, I would gladly have shared all of this with Miss Ortmann. My beginners, however, tend to have trouble with the question. "What music do you listen to?" I say, after they have been introduced to middle C and counted all the Cs on my piano. Usually, the answer is a blank stare. They don't know what music they listen to; they don't know that they listen to music.

And maybe they don't listen, but they do hear music. They hear it all the time. They hear it with every television commercial, every video game, every movie, every trip to the supermarket or the mall. They are literally bombarded with musical stimulation—but usually as accompaniment to a visual image or as part of a sell or, very often, both. Listening to music, as an activity sufficient unto itself, is something very few children have experienced in our visually overstimulated culture. So my first job is to rescue music from its ubiquity—to pull it from the background to the forefront, free it from its uses. "What's your favorite movie, Jenny?" I ask when she assures me she never listens to music. "*Harry Potter*," she says instantly. I play her the first phrase of "Hedwig's Theme," a tune from the soundtrack. She is startled. Shaken loose from larger-than-life cinematic imagery and played on the austere geography of the black and white keys, the melody emerges as something simply to listen to. "Play it again," she says. I play it again. No flying brooms, no charismatic wizards, nothing at all to look at. Jenny sits, listening.

"What's your parents' favorite song?" can work too, for younger children especially. Maggie, for example, a round-faced eight-year-old, can recite all the lyrics of "Here Comes the Sun," including the exact number of repetitions of "Sun, sun, sun, here it comes." And Jenny knows every word of Abba's "Dancing Queen." They live with music; they've just never been conscious of hearing it.

Some beginners come with more awareness. "I listen to my brother's heavy metal," they tell me, or "I listen to *The Phantom of the Opera*" (as if it were a genre all its own, which perhaps it is). "I listen to jazz," says the son of a professional trombonist. He sighs. "All the time."

A lucky few come singing. Rebecca, for example, nine years old and Broadway-smitten, insists on ending lessons by reversing seats with me and singing "Where Is Love?" or "Castle on a Cloud" to my accompaniment. She tends to sing, in fact, all the way through her lessons; when she plays a melody without singing it, she says, "I can't hear it." This orientation may become problematic when she gets around to playing a Bach invention. For now, it is a distinct advantage: it helps her understand pitch direction. The business of pitches being higher or lower in relation to each other is trickier than one might think. Upon hearing two pitches within fairly close range, many young children can't tell which is higher. And certainly there's nothing intuitive about the layout of the keyboard, no logical or instinctive way to guess that moving to the right means going up in pitch and moving to the left, going down. But Rebecca can feel "up" and "down" in the tension and release of her vocal cords. As a result, she can learn and remember long melodies by ear. It's a rare gift; most young children have very little relationship with their singing voices.

Or, for that matter, with their fingers. They've lost some ground from their toddler years, when picking things up and manipulating them was such a monumental part of a day's work. My second task, then, is to get them reacquainted with their ten fingers.

Willy came to me at the age of seven with both hands

balled into tight fists. During his first lesson the pointer finger of each hand was reluctantly released from its fist. For an entire year—through his first lesson book, through Hanukah and Passover, through recital season—Willy played with those two fingers, and only those two. I despaired. I apologized to his parents, who were somewhat less upset than I thought they should be. "It'll work out," said his father.

Around October of his second year of lessons, Willy decided he wanted to learn to play "The Long and Winding Road." I mentioned that it would be easier if he used a few more of his fingers. Over the next few weeks, like slow-blooming flowers, Willy's fists began to open. Within a couple of months he could play a rousing rendition of "The Long and Winding Road" involving pinkies, thumbs, ring fingers, the works. "The Beatles would be proud," I told him.

"The Beatles are, like, over," he pointed out. "My dad's proud, though."

With fingers or with fists, singing or silent, all beginners come with excitement, and all come with apprehension. When they sit on my piano bench for the first time and take in the wide toothy smile of my Steinway grand, I can practically hear their hearts thudding in their ears. They have no idea what I will expect of them, or whether they will measure up. Frequently, they've forgotten why they wanted to do this in the first place. They wonder when the lesson will be over, and whether their mother will forget to pick them up. They wonder who gets to eat the jellybeans in the dish on the shelf behind them. (Miss Ortmann would probably be appalled about the jellybeans. I am waiting for the day a parent becomes appalled, for hygienic reasons, but there have been no epidemic outbreaks as of this writing.)

Occasionally—not often, but it happens—the first-lesson apprehension is overpowering. I think of Robert, whose mother is a friend of mine and had assured me for months that he was dying to take lessons. When she dropped him off at my house for the first time and I escorted him to the piano, he sat on the bench and directed his gaze away from me and out the window. No matter what I said to him, he did not respond or move. His face, as he studied my rhodo-dendron, was completely impassive. Five minutes went by, ten minutes; my chipper attempts to make conversation fal-tered. "Robert, is there anything I can do to make you com-fortable?" Not a move, not a flicker. "Well, then," I said briskly, "I'll leave you for a few minutes and let you collect yourself." I understood that there would be no collecting, that he was literally paralyzed with anxiety. But what was I to do? I walked away from him, into my kitchen, and counted slowly to one hundred. Then I went back. I have known a great many small children, and I have never seen one sit still for so long. We sat still, finally, together.

After a very long time, the thirty minutes were up and my friend returned. "How was the lesson, honey?" she asked.

Robert slid off the piano bench. "Fine," he said.

"I just knew you'd love it," she told him, beaming, and home they went from Robert's first, and last, piano lesson.

Usually, however, the first lesson really is fine: I make it my business to see that all goes well. We find middle C, we locate the seven other Cs, we wiggle fingers one by one and identify each as number one, two, three, four or five. We talk about what they do or don't listen to. We spend some time petting Joey, the very small beagle who rules my household. We each have a jellybean. I teach the child how to play the beginning of a tune—"Hot Cross Buns," or "Frère Jacques," or "Mary Had a Little Lamb."

That, of course, is the high point of the lesson—and perhaps the moment of least complicated pleasure in some students' entire musical careers. "Mommy, I can play the first six notes of 'Three Blind Mice'!" The difference between being able to play nothing on the piano and being able to play something—even a very small something—is enormous. The child may never again close a gap quite so wide.

The elation usually continues for a few more lessons. We learn where D is, where E is. We learn a few more notes of "Three Blind Mice." We become acquainted with the contours of a quarter note, a half note. More jellybeans, more cuddles with Joey. In good time, F, G, A and B make an appearance. If they really beg me, I allow them (forgive me, Miss Ortmann) to play "Chopsticks" at the end of a lesson. Mothers remember to come back. Apprehension begins to subside.

But at some point during the early lessons—the point varies from child to child, but it never fails to arrive—a beginning student will come to the dismaying realization that at the piano, play is serious. Play, in fact, is work. Invariably, at some point, the cry goes up: "It's hard!"

It is hard. There is no magic jellybean antidote for this. Playing with one hand is hard; playing with two hands at the same time is very hard. Playing with several different fingers of two hands at once is close to impossible. Ask Willy.

Coordinating hands, eyes and ears is hard. Looking at the written music means missing the correct keys. Looking at your hands means losing your place in the written music. I have seldom had a beginning student who did not at some point become confused about which staff is for which hand. I think of Damian, who over the course of several weeks learned to play a simple rendition of "The Pink Panther" with great enthusiasm. It was hard, all right, but he could do it. Then came spring vacation, and I did not see him for several weeks. When he came back, he was despondent; "The Pink Panther" didn't sound right. I asked him to play it for me. He stared hard at the music and played an odd hiccupping version of the bass pattern in his right hand, a mangled melody in his left. He had simply forgotten which hand was supposed to play which part of the music.

Mastering musical time is hard. It's curious to me why this should be; after all, each of us lives with—and lives by—the most profoundly constant, steady beat imaginable. And yet the absolute rule of organized beats that characterizes musical time is something even talented children find difficult to grasp. It is not easy to explain, even to a talented child, that once he starts playing a piece of music he has no choice about when he plays each note. Musical time does not stop and wait for him to ruminate, dawdle, follow a whim. He may be in a hurry to get to the end of a song, but he is not at liberty to speed up. Musical time demands submission.

And even when a child has grasped the inexorability of the musical beat, then there is the matter of how beats are organized—usually in groups of two or in groups of three. Overwhelmingly, students have a natural tendency toward duple meter; my guess is that this is because we have two legs and so walk in duple meter. When playing their first pieces in triple meter—that is, with beats organized as "one-two-three, one-two-three," and so on—they will almost invariably turn the three beats into four (a multiple of two, hence duple) by playing "one-two-three-*pause*, one-two-three-*pause*." It's interesting that for the medieval monks who developed musical notation, triple meter, not duple, was the norm. A long note was considered "perfect" if it represented three beats—reflecting the perfection of the Trinity—and "imperfect" if it represented two. For my youngest students, three is not perfection. It's just hard.

And then there are rests, the fanciful marks on the staff that indicate the passing of a beat or beats with no note being played. With the appearance of a rest, the idea of a beat becomes even more elusive—not only invisible but inaudible. This is mystifying, for example, even to Mara, who is clearly a talented child. The daughter of a lawyer and a jazz singer, Mara has an agile mind and a pure, flute-like voice. But the appearance of a rest on the musical staff, at some point in the course of her early lessons, stops her in her tracks. "Doesn't a rest mean nothing?" she says. I try to explain. I make a guess that she's got a flair for math; I compare a rest in music to a zero in arithmetic. She listens, she nods her head; she plays the musical phrase again and plows right through the rest, just as she did before. I am stymied, and not for the first time. A rest is in fact mysterious. It holds a place and organizes everything around it, but it can't be heard; it's a silence with the heft and significance of sound.

Hardest of all, for most beginners, is learning to read musical notation—a system of signs and symbols that is miraculously efficient and dense with meaning, but not particularly child-friendly. The system acquired complexity as it evolved; it had to, in order to be able to represent the ever more complex forms and idioms of Western art music. As I struggle to teach this elegant and intimidating code, it occurs to me sometimes how much easier the earliest versions of notation would be for a child to grasp. They were nothing more than the graffiti of singers—specifically, those medieval monks, whose rituals of worship were dominated by the dark, floating melodies of Gregorian chant. For centuries the melodies were passed on through oral tradition, but sometime during the ninth century a clever monk here and there began to scribble little markings above the Latin words to help jog his memory. The earliest markings, called "neumes," were casual, whimsical fragments of curving line—like miniature versions of the marks on road signs that mean "zigzags ahead." They didn't indicate specific pitch at all, but simply pitch direction. With no specification of this or that note, no indication of rhythm or meter, they served merely to remind the singer, "When you sing 'Alleluia' your voice should go higher here, lower there." It is fascinating to try to imagine the process of trial and error through which, when Frère François and Frère Pierre sang at Mass, they managed to stay together.

As the chants grew longer and more complex, the neumes began to accrete small thickenings at the beginning, middle and end of a curve, indicating arrival at pitches. And at some point a monk who was particularly clever, or fastidious, or both, drew a horizontal line, representing a fixed pitch, around which the tendrils of his neumes could curl and cling. The five lines and four spaces of our musical staff, as well as all the trappings of rhythm and meter, took hundreds of years more to develop.

Thinking about the fanciful doodles of the monks, I've imagined a pedagogy that doesn't begin with lines and spaces and clefs at all, or even with the piano keys, but starts simply with drawing little lines curving up and down and then singing them. Maybe for "Alleluia" we could substitute "macaroni." Once the concept of higher versus lower was mastered, we could gradually add pitches, then a horizontal line, then another. Could we, I wonder, duplicate the centuries-long evolution of musical notation in a fast-forward fashion? If we began in September, could we be ready to read music in time for "Jingle Bells" and "The Dreidl Song"?

Well, it's a theory. I've never had the nerve to try it. After all, parent and child have signed up for piano lessons, not chicken scratchings and macaroni. So I teach them—slowly—to read notes the conventional way.

Decoding the notes in one clef is hard enough. When the realization sinks in that notation in the treble clef is different from notation in the bass clef, the almost universal response is "That's not fair!" Why can't a G in the bass clef be written like a G in the treble clef, Maggie demands indignantly, as though it's my fault.

There is an answer to this, of course. On the bass clef

staff, notation is located so that most of the notes within the range of lower-pitched instruments and voices will be written on the lines and in the spaces of the staff; the same rule applies to the treble clef staff and higher-pitched instruments and voices. Maggie is not impressed by this explanation. She decides to stage a protest, and for a few weeks, until the dissonances grow unbearable, she plays all the bass clef notes as though she were reading treble clef. "Maggie," I say, "you have to learn to read bass clef."

"It's hard," she says.

It *is* hard. Mistakes are constant. Confusions abound. When confronted with a challenge that feels too great, my more resourceful beginners look for ways to avoid it. They will begin doing backbends off the piano bench or cracking their knuckles. The smallest ones will crawl into my lap and close their eyes. More sophisticated students try to distract me. "Did you watch the Yankee game last night?" they will ask brightly, or "Did you know that my birthday is in two months and twelve days?" Maybe she'll just forget about eighth notes, they are thinking. Mara, up against a ¾ time signature for the first time, watches my left hand intently as I demonstrate the accompaniment to a waltz. "One-two-three, one-two-three—do you understand how it goes, Mara?" I say, encouraged by her focused attention. She wrinkles her nose. "You have lots of vines in your hands," she remarks. "Is that 'cause you're old?"

It flashes through my mind that one of Mara's enduring, indelible memories of her piano lessons will be the vines in my hands. With an effort, I manage to work my way past this. "Three-quarter time is hard, right, Mara?" I say, and she nods mournfully.

It is all hard. Therefore every small triumph, in this beginning period, is an occasion for celebration. One-two-three, one-two-three . . . Mara manages not to insert an extra beat between two measures. Eureka!

Willy uncurls his ring finger and plunks it on a key. Eureka!

Jenny stares at a note. "So if that one is E, then that one is . . ." Her lips are parted. She's not breathing. She takes a chance. "That one is F?" Eureka, for sure.

Oddly enough, for me these triumphs are not entirely uncomplicated. When I teach beginners, here is what I find hard: knowing that sometimes the acquisition of a musical skill comes at the expense of a musical impulse.

Most children, after all, approach the piano initially with some degree of spontaneous pleasure. They play random streams of notes, knotty chord clusters, tolling low notes with the pedal clamped down. They are enjoying pure sonority. The piano is inviting that way: unlike a flute or a violin, it will make a pleasant sound for anyone, anytime. And the more gifted children are, the more they love to play around on the keys.

As a teacher, I find this both a delight and a challenge. Ideally, I want to preserve the playful impulse, to align the lessons along its grain. But alas, much of what I have to teach will necessarily suppress it. Reading notes, counting beats, figuring out rhythms—in the course of concentrating on these arduous tasks, the spontaneous behavior often goes underground. Unless I remember to dig for it now and then, it may never reemerge.

There is a chapter in one of the *Mary Poppins* books wherein the Banks twins celebrate their first birthday. They have spent the first year of life lying in their cribs and carrying on fond, lively conversations with the starling who perches on the nursery windowsill. But gradually, of course, they have also begun to acquire human language. And when the starling shows up to wish them a happy birthday, he is heartbroken to discover they can no longer understand him. They are becoming socialized, civilized; but they have lost their untutored intimacy with the natural world. It's a necessary trade-off, of course; there's no way around it. One must master human speech in order to be competent in the world. But it's sad to lose the starling.

I think of that trade-off sometimes as I watch Mara learn to count beats, Damian try to match a hand with each clef, Jenny decipher the note on the second line. I know what they're gaining. I wonder what it's costing them. Don't I recall that Mara, at her earliest lessons, played haphazard, wandering melodies up and down the keys, before her coat was off? Didn't Damian occasionally produce great crashing chords with both hands at once, before he learned to read notes on staffs? Have we lost the silly melodies and the growling chords for good? And does it matter?

When I was five, my family relocated for a year from Baltimore to Philadelphia and rented a furnished house. There I made my first acquaintance with a piano. I played it often, knowing nothing, simply loving the sound of it. I composed a long and infinitely malleable piece and titled it, quite brilliantly I thought, *In the Moonlight*. My parents were appropriately impressed. At home in Baltimore the following year, I was overjoyed when a tremendous object wrapped in thick blankets appeared in the living room the week before Christmas. "Don't look under the blankets," said my mother. I was, in fact, able to wait until she went back to the kitchen before I crawled under the blankets and huddled there, stroking the three cold, shiny pedals, inhaling the scent of the cherry wood. On Christmas morning I played an especially elaborate and adrenaline-laced version of *In the Moonlight*.

The lessons with Miss Ortmann followed in due course. I learned to sit up straight, curve my fingers, play a scale, count eighth notes. I learned to play "Jingle Bells," "Yankee Doodle," "When the Saints Go Marching In." Along the way, and without anyone noticing, *In the Moonlight* quietly disappeared.

Did it matter? Not to Miss Ortmann, I'm sure. But I think it was a loss when my improvisatory impulse flickered and died. Like the Banks twins losing an ear for the meaning in a bird's song as they learned human speech, I lost my ear for my own wild, unschooled interior music as I acquired musical skills. This is not to say that I could or would have been a gifted improviser or composer; there was nothing especially original about my pianistic rambling. But it was mine.

So I try, now and then, to sustain or revive my young students' capacity for spontaneous play. Sometimes at the end of lessons we play thunderstorms, or waterfalls, or bike rides. Sometimes I play some nonsense and ask them to answer me, or to imitate me. When I turn the tables and tell them to play something for me to imitate, the little ones are always determined to play something I won't be able to re-produce and are thus inspired to play great, messy splatters of notes, flying free for a moment of beats and clefs and finger numbers.

Eureka, then, too.

For a shy beginner, of course, these flights of musical mayhem can be more intimidating than the work of learning where A is. Ella, for example, squirms when I ask her to play me some thunder. She would much rather play me a scale. Fair enough; she plays a lovely, meticulous scale. But every now and then I put her very briefly back on the hook. Ella is a bright child with a lively mind and a strong musical impulse; who knows when fear may give way to a sudden eruption of nerve?

Whether it's improvising or reading, counting rests or coordinating hands, nearly every lesson in the beginning stages involves a movement from fear to courage, from confusion to clarity. It may be very small. But it happens, almost always. And it is from these small, tremendous movements that the particular intimacy of the piano lesson is born. For me to witness that step over and over again—and for a student to trust me enough to let me witness it—is necessarily to create an intense connection.

It's a connection painters love to try to capture. I know of at least eight paintings titled *The Piano Lesson* or something similar—I'm sure there are more—and they are all remarkable in the intensity of feeling they evoke. In Renoir's version, a woman in a flowing orange dress leans over a girl seated at a piano, also dressed in flowing orange; the standing woman's arm is around the girl in a loving, protective gesture. On the top of the piano is a vase of brilliant flowers. A painting by Caillebotte conveys a more sisterly intimacy; two women, both dressed in black, are shown from the back, their faces obscured, so that it is hard to tell which is the teacher, which the student. One wears a hat, the other has a hand lifted. They stare intently at the sheet music on the piano rack. There is real heat in their closeness, their merged attention. There are flowers on the piano.

Francis Day's painting has a lovely young teacher on the piano bench with an excited little student behind her; it has the distinct feel of a mother showing her daughter how to play. The child's hands are poised in the air, fingers outstretched; she can hardly wait to give it a try. Yes, there are flowers on the piano.

In paintings by Muschamp and Muenier, teacher and student are not physically so close. Muschamp's teacher sits in a chair apart from the piano and tilts her head at an angle back toward her student. The teacher's face is rapt; the student's body leans toward the teacher as she plays. Through the music, clearly, they are touching. Flowers? Of course.

In Muenier's *The First Piano Lesson* the flowers are great white roses, and they are atop a clavichord. A very little girl sits at the keys, her feet swinging from the bench just like my Jenny's do, her hair done up in two little pigtails with black bows not unlike the way Jenny's hair is often held captive. She is paying no attention to the very large music book open on the rack; her left hand perches idle above the keys while she watches the fingers of her right tinkle the high notes. On a chair in the corner lies her beribboned hat; to her left, facing us and watching her, sits the teacher. This time it's a man, an old man, with wisps of white hair and an elegant cravat. He is not smiling. But his mild, affable expression is the essence of patience. The rectangle of sunlight beneath the little girl's dangling feet, from a window we can't see, gives the scene the feeling of a blessing.

Several twentieth-century masters ring interesting changes on the Impressionists' idyllic vision. Romare Bearden's *Piano Lesson (Hommage à Mary Lou)* is rendered in his jazz-inflected collage style, brimming with bright colors and bold lines, but his image of the teacher-student connection closely echoes that of Renoir. A black girl sits at a blue and green upright piano, which slants across the foreground of the picture; a black woman dressed in a golden blouse, a pink sash and a flowing skirt leans over her so that their heads are almost touching. The girl's hands are splayed crookedly, unworkably, across the keys. But she will learn. We know this, because the teacher's hand rests on her shoulder, a soft breeze blows green curtains away from a window full of blue sky, and on the piano next to a metronome and a drumstick sits—well, it's a plant, with curling green leaves. The painting is full of light and air, and tenderness.

All of these paintings, in fact, are replete with tenderness. All of them capture the moment of trust and acceptance at the heart of the lesson, the heart of the relationship.

Then there is Matisse's *Piano Lesson*. Of the student we see only his round child's face, staring at an open book of music; behind him, in a gray background of indeterminate distance, the faceless figure of a thin woman sits on a high stool. In a particularly violent gesture, a sharp black triangular wedge replaces one of the boy's eyes. The child's feeling of vulnerability, the teacher's aloofness and literal hauteur, are as intense and palpable as are the feelings of loving intimacy evoked by the other paintings.

There are no flowers on this piano.

It is interesting that in every one of the works depicting the piano lesson as tender communion, the students are female, as are most of the teachers. The male painters of these images were limning a scene they had not themselves experienced. But in Matisse's picture, where fear of humiliation dominates, the student is a boy. That black triangle across his face is like a spike of panic striking deep into the center of his psyche. One must wonder about Matisse's piano teacher.

I myself, in fact, have been a piano teacher in a painting. Seven-year-old Rosie was brought to her lessons by her grandmother, who was a painter of some local renown. Rosie was a cherubic child, blond and blue-eyed. "I want to learn 'Folsom Prison Blues,' " she announced early on. Well, of course. In the weeks that followed, as I attempted to teach Rosie how to play a blues riff or two, her grandmother sat in the next room and sketched us at work. "I can do something with this," she told me, which was more than I could honestly say about Rosie and the blues.

Some years later, long after Rosie had given up on Johnny Cash in particular and the piano in general, I happened to be talking to the mother of one of my preteen students, Stephanie, about her recent Bat Mitzvah. "I got her the best present," the mother told me excitedly. "I found this wonderful painting in the art gallery downtown—it's a little blond girl having a piano lesson. And the best part is that the teacher in the painting actually looks a little bit like you!"

I have never seen the painting, and wonder where it is now; Stephanie still takes lessons, but I would guess she is far too old and too cool to have a painting of a piano lesson hanging in her room. It's possible, though, that it reminds her of her own experience with the risky, vulnerable business of beginning piano lessons.

Now it is Jenny who is my most "beginning" student. I see her flinch as I turn the page in her lesson book to a piece called "Go for the Gold." "It's too hard," she says instantly.

"Why do you think so?"

"It's too black," she says.

It is very black. I have a sudden vivid recollection of my first recital piece, entitled "To a Wigwam." It was the last and most densely note-populated—hence the blackest—piece in my John Thompson primer book. I can still picture the music exactly—the dark, bristly repeated fifths in the left hand, the solemn whole notes in the right, the line drawing of the wigwam at the top of the page, complete with befeathered Indian dancers. I remember my dismay at learning it was to be my recital piece, and my pride when I eventually mastered it. Watching Jenny, I am seized with a desire for her to experience this transformation. "Just try to figure out the first right-hand note," I encourage her, but her anxiety is already running high. Brow furrowed, she plunks her right thumb down hard.

"It's not a D, Jenny," I tell her. The weather on her face changes from worry to confusion, then to concentration, and back to confusion again as she stares at the page. Do I want to know this much about this child? I have no choice. But it's not comfortable.

"What is it, then?"

I am silent. Jenny fidgets on the bench, squints her eyes, licks her lips. She moves her thumb to C, plays it as if by accident and shoots me a quick look. "Good, Jenny," I say, and the sun shines.

Miss Ortmann had a large and elegant room at the back of her Baltimore row house, a vast sort of parlor with a concert grand in a bay window, which she used for her recitals. I remember the room only dimly, but I know exactly what I wore for that first recital: a magical outfit that came in two parts, a sheer pink dress with a translucent green embroidered smock worn over it and tied with a sash. The green smock, my pink barrettes, and the roar of dark sound when I played those drum-like fifths on that great piano with its top up—in my memory, that was the recital. Did anyone else play? I suppose so.

Jenny plays the low C at the end of "Go for the Gold" and exhales at long last. I offer her a jellybean. "You know, you'll play that really well if you practice it," I say. "You could play it in the recital."

The jellybean stops halfway to her mouth. "What recital?"

I explain to her that every June I hold a recital, and that all of my students play for one another and their parents, and that it's very exciting, and that she'll do a great job.

"Uh-uh," she says.

"Everybody plays," I tell her.

"Not me." The jellybean is chomped. I stare at her, impressed by her utter assurance. I can picture her, though, in green embroidery and pink barrettes. "Can we play 'Chopsticks' now?" she says, and so I yield and end the lesson with "Chopsticks" as Miss Ortmann twirls, I am sure, gracefully and rhythmically in her grave.

CHAPTER TWO

The Pull of Pop

*D*amian has a new iPod. He is ten years old, and very proud. He brings his iPod to a piano lesson, and before he is willing to open his lesson book to "Song for A Scarecrow," he needs to play me something. We hook up his iPod to my speakers and we listen. "Playas everywhere.... Pimp on, pimp on, pimp on . . ." Damian gives me the smile of an angel. After all, I have been encouraging him to become aware of what he listens to. "Can you teach me to play that?" he asks.

We live in a pop-saturated world. Damian's world, specifically—the world of a preteen suburban African-American boy in a metropolitan area—is saturated with hip-hop. Damian hears it in the television ads he watches, in the malls where he shops, in the movies he sees. It emanates from his brother's stereo system and his sister's friends' car radios. We may immerse ourselves in "Song for a Scarecrow" on Saturday mornings, but music for Damian, seven days a week, is hip-hop.

For a piano teacher, this is no small problem. The particular virtues of the piano are utterly irrelevant to the vast majority of rap music; I may as well be teaching Damian to play cathedral chimes. Hip-hop is all about the spoken word and the electronically rendered beat. There is no place for a piano here.

It's impressive, actually, what a departure even from traditional pop this music represents. There is frequently no melody; harmonic movement is minimal and sometimes nonexistent. The very vocabulary used to talk about the music is different: in the hip-hop industry the word "beat" means not the metric pulse of the music, but the particular hook or groove around which a song (well, a cut) is built. Even more peculiar, to my ear, is that the act of creating one of these cuts often doesn't seem to involve anyone referred to as a songwriter. There is an artist, who raps (more often than not, he writes his own words); and there is a producer, who conceives the feel, the mood, the "beat" of the piece, and who assembles the digital sounds required to realize his concept. Do you see a songwriter in this picture? I don't. And I certainly don't see a boy at a piano.

But here is Damian at my piano, and this is what is on his iPod. I can give him my first, visceral response, and tell him that the song we just listened to represents the antithesis of the values—musical, aesthetic, even moral—to which I have devoted my life. Or I can spare him that bit of news, and try to meet him halfway. His face is eager, expectant. We listen again. I discover that there is a thudding bass line consisting of a series of notes in a repeated rhythmic figure (this, you understand, is the beat). I teach him the notes. He is elated; he thinks he has learned the song. Maybe he has.

I have no interest in deploring hip-hop as a genre. As difficult as it can be for me to listen to, I recognize that it is a powerful and original development in the worldwide evolution of popular music. It has reasserted the primacy of rhythm in Western music, and has natural links with rhythm-dominated music of other cultures. It has stimulated the invention of new electronic sounds. And it represents something genuinely new in the relation of words to music. Whether I like it or not, I can see that it has become the global language of pop.

Besides, both of my sons listen to it. They are doing their best to educate me as to good hip-hop and bad, and to point out that there is plenty of clever, appealing, subversive and passionate hip-hop to be heard. I'm paying attention. But as a piano teacher, I'm stumped. There's nothing here I can teach.

Other varieties of mainstream pop music are nearly as problematic. It's bad enough that much of the music that dominates the airwaves seems to me at best inane, at worst meretricious. What's even more dispiriting for a piano teacher is that some genres have done away with instruments altogether. Electronic dance music, for example, is created from digital samples and drum machines—and turntables, in the hands of the DJs who have achieved the status of creators in this genre. Asking a pianist to try to render this music is like asking him to reproduce the sound of a pneumatic drill. And while electronic dance music is at the extreme end, many other kinds of pop music rely increasingly on sampling and digital editing software; even the singer's voice is often heavily processed and sometimes sampled, becoming just another element in the wash of electronic sounds.

There are, of course, plenty of pop songs that still use instruments. Those instruments, however, are more likely to be guitars than pianos. And those songs are more likely than not to be harmonically static, melodically uneventful, lyrically bombastic and overwhelmed by percussion—drop out the rhythm track and you have the bare shadow of a song.

Willy is eleven now—with all ten fingers in good working order—and he has an iPod, too. The song he wants to play for me is by the band Metallica. We connect to my stereo and listen to a series of guitar chords that sound to me like successive head-on automobile collisions. There is a male voice singing or shouting, but nothing is intelligible except for the single word *"Whiplash!"* Willy's head is bobbing rapturously up and down to the beat. "Whiplash!" he chimes in. "Whiplash!" He glances at me. "Can you teach me this?" His smile is as endearing as Damian's.

"Whiplash!" sings, or yells, the male voice. There isn't even a distinctive bass line here to attend to. I call to Willy above the din. "What do you like about this song?"

He looks startled. "I don't know," he allows, "it's just—it's just—" His head is bobbing away. It occurs to me that it's all about the head-bobbing, the sheer pulsing energy in the music that somehow matches what is going on inside an eleven-year-old boy. I turn the volume down on my stereo system. With a flick of his thumb he turns it back up again on the iPod. The guitar assault escalates from car crash to artillery fire. I gaze at the serene black and white calligraphy of my Steinway keys. It is tempting to despair.

I turn my stereo volume down again, this time all the way. Silence spreads across my piano studio, sweeter than a Mozart sonatina. Willy's head jerks to a stop. "Willy," I say, "what else do you have on your iPod?"

This, it turns out, is an interesting question. It so happens that Willy's iPod contains not only Metallica and 50 Cent, but also a wildly eclectic mix of other genres and styles, from Dave Matthews's 1990s hit "Satellite" to a Broadway show tune called "Oh, the Things You Can Think!" (from a musical based on the writings of Dr. Seuss), and pretty much everything in between. If a time traveler picked up Willy's iPod to discover what pop music sounded like in the first years of the third millennium, he would be very confused.

This is what I find most interesting about contemporary pop: it has many, many faces. Certainly, the most commercial genres dominate, but a vast array of other genres thrives more modestly alongside them: solo singer-songwriters with acoustic guitars, jam bands with tie-dyed guitar straps, funk bands and teen crooners and Latin heart-throbs all command followings of respectable size and passionate devotion. I once asked the students in a college music appreciation course I taught to list all the genres of popular music they knew about. Firing categories at me faster than I could write them on the board, they came up with this list: rap, hip-hop, gangsta rap, rock, alternative, reggae, jazz, jam rock, acoustic rock, funk, grunge, folk, nature music, heavy metal, blues, R&B, country, Latin, reggaeton, bluegrass, world music, show music, ska, punk, emo, hardcore, drum-and-bass, soul, neo-soul, disco, trance, house, techno and gospel. "There's a lot more," said a student apologetically at the end of class. "I can't believe that's all we could think of."

Pop music has always come in more than one flavor, of course, but it seems hard to imagine that anyone could have come up with a list of similar length in the 1920s, or the 1940s, or the 1970s for that matter. As a young teenager, I could choose between Janis Joplin and Herman's Hermits; my mother at a similar age could choose between Bing Crosby and Artie Shaw; but Willy can spin the magic wheel of his iPod and choose between punk and funk and grunge and house and emo and techno . . . and let's not forget Dr. Seuss.

Isn't it odd that this fragmentation of the pop music world has occurred as corporate control of media has become more and more centralized? It would seem almost inevitable that with the tendency toward ever-greater industry consolidation, commercial music would become steadily more homogenized, more standardized. During the dance music craze of the late 1990s, media pundits assured us that DJs were on the way to replacing instrumentalists, for better or worse, and forever. And in the face of the recording industry's relentless packaging and marketing of celebrity performers like Britney Spears and the winners of *American Idol*, music critics have frequently foretold an imminent future when all pop will sound the same: glossy, soulless and mechanized.

And yet something else seems to be happening: genres and styles are proliferating rather than being squeezed out of the marketplace. What the pundits of the 1990s didn't take into account was the titanic effect the Internet would have on the way music can be marketed and distributed. The Internet loves a niche. Any musician with a recording and a website to her name can connect with and build a fan base; any net-surfing twelve-year-old can locate a musician in any genre and then find other offerings in that genre. I have ceased to be amazed at the Internet savvy of my students, even the youngest ones; now I'm simply impressed by the variety of pop music they bring to their piano lessons.

Let me clarify: they do this at my request. Call me a glutton for punishment, but I sometimes ask my students to bring me recordings of the pop music they listen to. When the music they bring me is even remotely playable on the piano, I help them figure out how to play it. For beginners, this usually amounts to picking out the tune. More developed students will be able to add chords and some kind of rhythmic feel.

I encourage this partly because it can help motivate students to practice. A child who just can't get himself to the piano every day in order to master Clementi may find his way there more easily if he can bang out the melody to Green Day's latest anthem. And once he's reached saturation with Green Day, he might even take a look at Clementi.

More important, I like to include popular music in lessons because I think it's important for kids to learn to play by ear as well as from written notation. Hip-hop and heavy metal notwithstanding, there are still many varieties of pop music that lend themselves well to this project—tunes with clear, simple harmonies and symmetrical melodic phrases. Tunes with words, an obvious but critical advantage: you can almost always remember a melody if you know the words to it. Then, too, it's easier to play a tune by ear if you're very familiar with it. And when a student brings me a favorite pop tune, chances are he's very, *very* familiar with it; if you've ever taken a long car ride with a young child, you know that children listen to songs they like on an average of two or three hundred times in a row. "Willy," I say, "do you like the Dave Matthews song 'Satellite'?"

His eyes light up; I watch him forget about Metallica. "I *really* like it," he says, "I listen to it all the time." Well, then. We have something to work with.

We begin by listening. "Satellite" starts with a twelve-note phrase played by the solo guitar four times in a row, the fourth time breaking off abruptly in the middle. I teach Willy the twelve notes. It's in the key of A flat, which means lots of back-and-forth between white and black keys. This requires some navigational dexterity, but after several tries he manages to play it very slowly. The phrase is too angular and jagged to be called a melody—its leaps between pitches make it virtually unsingable—but its spacey beauty is instantly appealing. Part of the appeal is the enigmatic quality of the rhythm. The notes are all even (one would write them as eighth notes, probably) and it's hard to tell how the twelve notes are subdivided; that is, where the accents are, and where the beats fall. "When you play those notes, how are you counting in your head?" I ask Willy.

He looks bewildered; of course he's not counting at all. I don't blame him. It's impossible to guess where the beats are, but because of the pitch patterns, I hear it initially like this: *one-two-three, one-two, one-two, one-two-three*. Dave Matthews meets Igor Stravinsky? It's captivating but very irregular, very odd. When the guitar breaks off in the middle, the fourth time, it's as though the rhythmic peculiarity has gotten the better of it. It's gotten the better of Willy, too; he can't begin to count the weird accent pattern I've come up with. But he is fascinated when I do it. The guitar seems to decide to give it another try: the repeated phrase begins again, this time nudged by a second solo guitar. Three repetitions once again, and another break-off. The effect of rhythmic disorientation is stronger than ever. And now it comes again, but this time there is a violin too, playing a simple, staccato five-note countermelody, and with its help we hear the guitar phrase completely differently; now it's *one-two-three-four-five-six, one-two-three-four-five-six*. Two times six equal beats, then. Still too fast for Willy to count with me, but it's regular, and we begin to tap our feet. This is, after all, pop music; rhythmic eccentricity notwithstanding, one needs to tap one's foot at the very least, if not bob one's head. For the final time the guitar plays its four phrases; now the violin is in charge and the rhythm entirely clear, and now we don't hear each of the twelve eighth notes so distinctly; we notice only the six emphasized beats, and even those we now hear in two groups of three. Willy and I count together—*one-two-three, **one**-two-three*—and then we're not tapping anymore, we're swaying, because when beats are organized in groups of three and you don't know how to waltz, you sway: *one (two-three) one (two-three) one . . . one . . .* "Sing, Dave!" cries Willy.

"*Satellite in my eyes . . .*" They sing together, Willy and Dave. The jumpy, pointillistic twelve-note pattern continues underneath, but the drums kick in, and there's no choice but to sway. "*Like a diamond in the sky / How I wonder.*" Willy may not be consciously aware that the lyric quotes a nursery rhyme, but it's amazing how the infant resonance of that line deepens the song's evocation of a childlike comfort in mystery. The melody is a child's tune: a step down, a few steps up, back down again. I press the pause button on the iPod. "The first note he sings is a B flat," I tell Willy, "you take it from there."

"Satellite in my eyes," he sings to himself, poking at black and white keys. It doesn't take him long to figure out how to play the little tune. We listen to the next line. "*Satellite strung from the moon / And the world your balloon . . .*" Willy plays his four notes up and down again; he's able to hear that the same tune fits these new words.

"Winter's cold," sings Dave Matthews. It's a child's cry; he throws his voice up an octave so that the word "cold" is a high, icy filament of sound, brings it briefly down to sing *"spring erases,"* throws it back up again and keeps it there in the vocal high-wire act he's famous for. *"Winter's cold,"* keens Willy. I tell him to play a low A flat and then a high one and to listen to how an octave sounds. He plays the octave jump, he sings it, he plays it. *"Winter's co-o-o-l-d,"* he sings again, operatically. He's goofing off now; he's had enough for this session. I ask him if he remembers how to play the opening twelve-note pattern. He does. Home he goes, crooning *"Like a diamond in the sky . . ."* He will probably play the opening guitar riff and the beginning of the tune fifty times a day. His parents will probably wonder how it can be that he has nothing to show for a half-hour lesson but twelve notes and a kiddie tune.

The way I see it, though, Willy's half hour has been well spent. He's gotten under the skin of music he loves, and discovered a little about what it's made of and how it's put together. He's learned that finding and counting beats can be like a treasure hunt; sometimes you need a few clues. He's become familiar with playing in a key that uses an asymmetrical jumble of black and white notes, a key his lesson books won't introduce for another few years. And he's done all this by listening, and by playing, instead of by deciphering notes on a page.

Many of my students bring me Dave Matthews songs.

They like the combination of the driving rock-and-roll beat with the lush sounds of the violin and saxophone; they like the strange loveliness of the lyrics, so wide open to fabulous misinterpretation. Others bring me songs by John Mayer, their generation's answer to "Sweet Baby James" Taylor, or by the popular British group Coldplay. Younger kids bring me bubbly teen pop; older students sometimes bring me recordings of their favorite jam bands, who improvise on each tune for as long as ten or fifteen minutes (just try learning one of those by ear). The songs are as disparate as my students, but one thing is consistent: they bring me songs that have touched them somehow. For each child, something about the song—a lilting beat, a startling chord, a lyric she can trust, a melody with a catch in it—feels charged, and moves her in some way. This is the pull of a good pop tune: it taps into some strong current of emotion in an apparently artless way. Learning to play these songs can give children a powerful kind of access to their own deeply felt but inexpressible fears and loves and longings.

Susie, at nine the tiniest almost-teenager I know, loves the music of the made-for-TV movie *High School Musical* and wants to learn the movie's big romantic ballad, called "Start of Something New." I help her pick out the melody and teach her a few simple chords to play along with it. The song starts in the key of C and then modulates to D, which adds a nice pedagogical angle. When the love-struck high school boy and girl reach the syrupy chorus, they sing to each other in harmony; I teach Susie how to play both vocal lines on the piano and inform her that she's playing thirds, which sounds grown-up to her. As energetic as she is small, she perches at the very edge of the piano bench in order to reach the pedal as she plays emphatic chords with her left hand and negotiates those cool thirds with her right. Within a few weeks she can play the whole song perfectly. I expect her to be thrilled, but she gives me a preteen scowl. "We left out one of the words," she says.

"Which word, Susie?" I'm certain we've figured out the melody lines perfectly.

" 'Oo-oo,' " she says. "Like, there's all those places where they go 'oo-oo'? You left it out every time." She's right, of course. What was I thinking? In a teen pop ballad, "oo-oo" is probably the crucial lyric.

Many of my students' favorite pop tunes are songs from musicals; they like these songs not only because they are tuneful and infectious, but also because they are reminders of favorite dramatic moments and characters. Susie loves "Start of Something New" for its fluffy soft-rock feel, but she's also mystified and captivated by the romantic fantasy it evokes. My somewhat older student Sara loves "Popular," from the Broadway show *Wicked*, for similar reasons; the song transports her to the particular corner of Oz where the impossibly glamorous and charismatic good witch promises lessons in popularity. Sara is very busy addressing the complicated equations of early adolescence; she comes to her lessons in soccer shorts and dangly earrings, alternates between girlish giggles and a twenty-something cool, has a mouthful of braces and has recently straightened her hair. "Popular" is actually a satire about the vacuity of being popular; the satiric element, however, is entirely lost on a thirteen-year-old girl, for whom a promise of popularity is serious business indeed.

And then there is eleven-year-old Matthew, who loves every song from that grandfather of pop musicals, *The Phantom of the Opera*. Matthew has put together a medley of his favorite *Phantom* tunes, and I believe there have been nights when his parents have considered leaving home so that they do not have to hear Matthew's *Phantom* medley one more time. Matthew is a small, serious child with fleet fingers and a strong perfectionist impulse. I watch him sing under his breath as he plays "The Pha-a-a-a-n-tom of the Op-er-a is here, inside your mind!" and I am fairly sure that Matthew, pounding those repeated bass notes, *is* the Phantom right at this moment, free from strict parents and demanding teachers, tremendous and terrible to behold and powerful enough to take possession of a soprano's mind and bring down a chandelier.

Theater songs are performed, for the most part, by orchestras; Dave Matthews's songs and many of my students' other pop favorites rely primarily on the sounds of the guitar, bass and drums. Sometimes, though, students find their way through the alcoves and byways of the contemporary pop labyrinth to music that uses, of all things, the piano. Not the electric piano or the digitally sampled piano, mind you, but the antediluvian miracle of wood and felt and cast iron and steel string that stands in my piano studio. I, of course, am delighted when this happens.

Some of my teenage students love Vanessa Carlton, a young singer-songwriter who, like so many of her peers, is all long hair and inky mascara and attitude, with a breathy little-girl pout in her voice. Instead of the guitar, though, she plays the piano—and she really plays. Some are fascinated by Regina Spektor, whose pianism is nearly classical in its style and technical facility and whose free-associative lyrics constitute a wild and wayward poetry. Learning the piano part to her haunting *"Après Moi"* is every bit as strenuous and satisfying as learning a song by Schubert.

And some like Norah Jones, a pianist with a voice of honey and smoke, who came to prominence a few years ago with her languid ballad "Don't Know Why." The piano sound here is very different from that of *"Après Moi"*; Jones's solo seems to drip from her fingers, as though she might just drift off to sleep before she gets to the end of it. But it's bluesy and sensuous and easy to learn, and it teaches my teenagers that there is nothing on earth sultrier than a piano solo if only you play it slowly enough.

They are not all female, the new crop of piano-playing pop artists. Just this year my students have introduced me to piano-driven songs by two bands called Ben Folds Five and Five for Fighting, bands led by men with plaintive high voices and a deft touch on the keys. Both songs begin with meticulous, achingly sweet piano solos; in both, the lead sings alone over the rippling piano for a stanza or two before the rest of the band kicks in. One song is the tale of a romantic crisis, the other a meditation on the passage of time; both are pensive and poetic, their lyrics filled with loneliness and longing, hope and loss. "*Now that I've found someone,*" sings Ben Folds, "*I'm feeling more alone / Than I ever have before.*" "*There's never a wish better than this / When you only got one hundred years to live,*" goes the chorus of the Five for Fighting song. The words are effortlessly appealing to a sensitive teenager, but it's the piano parts, those spare, wistful arpeggios, that really speak to my students. From an instructional standpoint this is a happy circumstance, because the harmonies are so basic and so easy to hear. I can show Debbie, as we listen to the song "One Hundred Years," that these notes outline an A chord, these a D chord, these a B-minor chord, and she can see the architecture of the chords right there on the piano keys as she listens to the notes. "It's so simple," she says, "why is it so pretty?" I explain that the harmonies move away from the home chord of A and then back again, over and over, and that with every cycle there is an effect of tension followed by relief.

Debbie, who sometimes comes to lessons in her lacrosse uniform, has been studying with me for a long time. While her playing isn't flashy or technically advanced, there's an ease and fluency to it; she has made playing the piano a part of who she is. I would love to enlighten her on the mysterious and weighty question of what makes music pretty, but I can see from the blank look on her face that I haven't quite succeeded. "What's the prettiest part?" I ask her.

We listen again to the sequence of harmonies, and when she hears an E7 suspension chord at the end of a phrase, she says without hesitation, "Right there."

I give it another try. I tell her that in this key, E7 is the chord that tugs us urgently to the home chord; by definition, then, it's an unsettled chord, propelling the music forward. And when it occurs in an altered form called a suspension, one of its notes is replaced with a neighboring note, a kind of deliberate mistake in the heart of the chord that arouses our anticipation of the "wrong" note giving way to the right one. There are two tugs going on here, then: the tug of one note toward another, inside the chord, and the tug of the chord itself toward another chord.

So, I conclude, that's why it's so pretty.

Debbie looks politely mystified. "Yeah, right," she would say if she were not such a well-mannered girl. I've explained everything, and I've explained nothing. She knows what she feels when she hears that E7 suspension. And now she knows what it's made of. But the truth is that neither I nor anyone else can begin to answer the age-old question of why what it's made of makes her feel that way—why a displaced note and an unsettled chord can render her wide open to tenderness, sorrow, joy.

Not everyone would respond quite so strongly to that particular chord, of course. Children's responses to pop music can be every bit as individual as those of adults, and their tastes just as particular. "One Hundred Years" would do nothing for Matthew, my *Phantom* aficionado, just as "The Music of the Night" holds no interest for Debbie. What accounts for the astonishing diversity of taste and preference, even among people of similar age and cultural background? It's another age-old question, and equally unanswerable. Who knows why, exactly, an E7 suspension gives Debbie the shivers? Who can say why that octave leap in "Satellite" stirs Willy the way it does? The intersection of personality and musical taste is as mysterious as it is undeniable.

A couple of years ago some musicians with a technological bent decided to track down that intersection and tame it for marketing purposes. Calling themselves the Music Genome Project, they drew up a list of specific, identifiable attributes, or "genes," of musical style—"funky guitar licks," for example, or "Latin percussion track"—and then set about analyzing the genetic makeup, as it were, of thousands of popular songs. Go to their website and enter your favorite pop tune, and an instantaneous list of songs with similar "genomes" will be generated, providing you with an entire listening library you're supposedly guaranteed to like. *Et voilà!* No more mystery. Your carefully cultivated musical identity is nothing but a marketing profile.

Well, maybe. Here on my piano bench, the wildly idiosyncratic nature of musical taste does not seem all that amenable to scientific analysis. I think of Tom, the trombone player's son, who is bent upon learning "Buffalo Soldier" and "How Sweet It Is to Be Loved by You" at the same time. If Tom were to go to the Music Genome Project's website and type in "Buffalo Soldier," would the program in all its quantifiable wisdom suggest that he might like Marvin Gaye as well? Not a chance. There's simply no logical intersection between these two great songs. Tom, however, hopelessly ignorant of his genomic profile, persists in liking them both. Which means, of course, that Tom himself is the intersection.

The incorrigible idiosyncrasy of musical preferences means that I encounter a great deal of variety in the pop area of my teaching: I never know whether I will be asked to teach hip-hop or country, a funk groove or the *Rugrats* theme song. Remember, too, that my students' access is not only to the many varieties of contemporary pop music but also to the popular music of earlier eras. And I'm consistently surprised by how many of them are drawn to the pop music of their parents' generation—my pop, to be precise. I realized recently that in the course of a week's lessons I had explored the following songs: "Yellow Submarine," "Allentown," "Blowin' in the Wind," "Downtown," and "Brandy." There was a veritable jukebox of oldies in my head that week.

Sometimes my students' enthusiasm for the music of my youth surpasses even my own. While I loved the Grateful Dead once upon a time, I never devoted myself to learning "Box of Rain," as my student Margot has done. And I used to sing along with Joni Mitchell on "Chelsea Morning" (I let Joni take care of the high notes all by herself); sixteen-year-old Tara, though, has taught herself with my help to play the gorgeous and complicated "Blue," a song where folk meets Debussy. I had friends during my teenage years who avoided their math homework by learning "Stairway to Heaven" in its astonishing entirety; I tended to avoid math homework by sight-reading sonatas (this may sound loftier, but I got the same math grades they did). Thirty-five years later, though, I have finally caught up with "Stairway to Heaven," because Matthew wants to play it—and so does Margot, not to mention Tara. As I teach it to my eager students, phrase by phrase and section by section, I am impressed. There are sonatas that are not so well constructed.

It's not only my teenagers who like what one young stu-

dent calls "the olden goldies." There is little Rebecca, crooning "Oh, you know it sure is hard to leave here, Carey," with
no trouble at all on the high notes; littler Maggie, mouthing
the words as she plays "Here comes the sun, and I say"; lit-
tlest Jenny, playing "Dancing Queen," verses and all, with
exactly one finger, and with no mistakes.

Maybe it's a myth after all that each generation needs to
reject the preceding one's preferences and tastes. As much as
I enjoy them now, I distinctly remember having no use for
Frank Sinatra or Peggy Lee when I was a teenager; but my
sons sing along with "Sweet Home Alabama" and "Ramblin'
Man"—and they know the words as well as I do.

I can't help but wonder why my kids and my students
find it easy to embrace their parents' music in a way that we,
as children and teenagers, never did. Perhaps it's because the
rock-and-roll beat slammed into action in the fifties, right
between our parents' musical youth and our own. That beat
redefined the sound of pop music so completely that the two
generations thus divided found it difficult even to listen to
one another's music. Our own children, though, are on the
same side of the divide as we are. So it's easy for them to
hear and to "get" our music; it may sound antiquated, but it's
within the rhythmic universe they know.

That still doesn't answer the question, though, of why so
many children not only like oldies but actually prefer them
to today's hits. Is it simply because these songs are associated

with that much-romanticized cultural turning point, part rowdy rebellion and part communal epiphany, that the sixties represent in our collective memory? Or was the music of the sixties and seventies actually better than today's pop? My friend Andy, a fine amateur pianist and opinionated amateur cultural historian, says emphatically that it was. Those were the days, he says, when A & R men roamed the earth hunting for artists; those were the days when authenticity was valued and creativity rewarded. That's why songs of that era have become classics, just as the show tunes of the thirties, forties and fifties became standards. These days, pop music has given up on artistry and gone for the easy sell, meaning that there will be no classics from the nineties and the "aughts."

It's a tempting theory. I doubt, myself, whether it's really so easy to anticipate what music will fade away and what will endure. I think it's likely, in fact, that when little Willy is in his dotage, he will remember "Satellite" as a classic of his youth.

But I will venture to agree with Andy that there is a particular and distinct charm to the music and lyrics of our generation's best songs—an adventurousness and originality, an ability to be catchy and simple without resorting to cliché; above all, a transparency of mood and feeling. Which brings us, of course, to the Beatles.

My students love old songs and new songs, obscure novelties and current hits, but more than anything else they love Beatles songs. The enduring appeal of the Beatles is close to unfathomable even for one who grew up with them, as I did; but as I teach these songs over and over, to students young and old, male and female, I see more and more clearly why their appeal is so wide and so deep. From the bouncy early anthems of puppy love to the Day-Glo hallucinations of the later albums, they combine very particular sounds and images with a universal resonance. They encompass wildly different styles and evoke every conceivable mood—the sinister silliness of "Maxwell's Silver Hammer," the etched cameos of solitude in "Eleanor Rigby" and "Fool on the Hill," the jolly anxiety of "When I'm Sixty-Four," the tenderness of "I Will." Yet Beatles songs always sound, somehow, like Beatles songs. The harmonies are fairly conventional but are used in interesting and distinctive ways. The melodies are like no one else's melodies; they're always memorable and often strikingly beautiful. The bass riffs, for example those opening salvos for "Day Tripper" and "Come Together" that seem by now to be part of our brains' hardwiring, are unlike any other bass lines. And the tunes and lyrics match as though they were foreordained. Could there be any other way to sing "I heard the news today, oh boy"?

Somehow all these elements conspire in a way that creates direct access to feeling. Think of the beginning of "Yesterday." It's nothing but Paul's voice, a few spare guitar chords and the word itself, set to three notes that trace exactly the spoken cadence of the word. "*All my troubles seemed so far away* . . ." Such a universal lament, yet expressed so simply and along so wistful a strand of notes that the sadness feels new, and palpable. And then: "Oh, I believe in yesterday . . ." Four chords for just five words, and three of them are major; the song's mood lifts for a moment, in spite of the fact that it's only nostalgia we're resorting to.

Or think of "Penny Lane," with its almost cinematic lyrics. The neighborhood is sketched in brisk march time, acutely specific, utterly mundane—and then the chorus bursts upon the scene in its bright new key, a reminder of the well of deep feeling so tightly contained in the bustling, quotidian suburban world.

I think it's this more than anything else that appeals to kids: these songs evoke strong, direct feeling—but always with a light touch, without becoming maudlin or bombastic. This can be a great gift to children, who need ways to experience and express their intense emotions without embarrassment. I'm reminded particularly of two students in recent years, Stephanie and Monica, both of whom were soft-spoken, thoughtful girls with deep reserves of sweetness behind their reticence. As they approached adolescence, I worried that I was losing touch with them; Stephanie was clearly, if quietly, dissatisfied with the music in her lesson books, and Monica's curtain of straight dark hair inevitably hid her face from me as she played. Both stopped practicing the piano during that period and seemed on the verge of quitting.

But they both loved the Beatles. Stephanie frequently wore a T-shirt with a picture of the Fab Four on the front; she loved Paul the very most. Monica could recite every word of "Lucy in the Sky with Diamonds" and wore granny glasses like John's. I told both of them that for a while we would work on nothing but learning Beatles songs by ear. "Not even scales?" said Monica. Ah, she had me there. But her face was animated for the first time in months; she was practically smiling.

"Not even scales," I said. "For a while." Within a few months Monica could play perfect, idiomatic versions of "Strawberry Fields Forever," "Eleanor Rigby," "Sgt. Pepper's Lonely Hearts Club Band," and—her favorite, she said, because the words made her happy—"I Am the Walrus." Stephanie worked her way through "Yesterday," "Let It Be" and "While My Guitar Gently Weeps," palpably comforted by this state of perpetual musical melancholy. They were searching for very different versions of emotional release, and both found what they were looking for in the Beatles.

They were unaware that along the way, as it happened, they found some of what I was looking to teach them. They learned to map long melodies on the keys with their fingers; they learned to remember these melodies with their minds and muscles both. They learned about key signatures, and about some of the ways songs are put together.

They even learned a little about chords and harmony—though it is far harder to perceive a chord by ear than it is to hear a melody. Musicians identify chords by which scale step they're built on: if a chord is built on step one of the scale representing the song's key, it's called a I ("one") chord. A chord built on step two of the scale is a II chord, a chord built on the fourth step, a IV chord and so on. It's surprisingly difficult, I've found, to teach kids to hear the differences in sound between these chords, and to tell which is which. Even very musical students like Monica have difficulty with this. From time to time, however, I make a try at it. "Listen to the Beatles sing 'We hope you will enjoy the show,' " I say to Monica. "When they sing the word 'show,' do you hear a five chord or a one chord?"

"Wait, what?" says Monica. She gives me her most opaque look, which is saying something.

"The five chord wants to move," I tell her, "the one chord is satisfied. Which does that one sound like?"

"Wait, *what*?"

"Think of the five chord as orange," I try recklessly, "think of the one chord as brown. Does that help?"

"Not. At. All," she responds with alacrity.

Well, then. "It's a one chord, Monica," I say. Next time maybe I'll try a food analogy.

I am having to invent this area of my teaching; my own teachers never ventured here. They were ferocious musicians, all of them, and I imagine they were capable of identifying all kinds of complex harmonies by ear; but they never tried to communicate the mysterious way this is done, and they never, ever brooked the idea of a pop song in the piano studio. I, of course, never dared to ask for one. If memory serves me, the idea of doing so crossed my mind exactly once, when I was eleven and beginning to be aware of the existence of rock and roll. I was living at the time in West Virginia, where I took piano lessons from a woman of surpassing elegance named Elizabeth Witschey; she had beautiful white fingers, a lively smile and a Southern accent so genteel that it sounded to me like a sort of melted British accent, and—but wait. First, I should mention my grandmother.

My grandmother, who came along when my family moved from Baltimore to West Virginia, loved a good laugh and a good smoke and a cutthroat Canasta game; she played "When the Saints Go Marching In" on some indeterminate sort of horn when she marched with the Baltimore chapter of the Ladies' Oriental Shrine, and could deliver a soul-stirring version of "In the Good Old Summertime" on the piano, by ear no less. My two younger sisters and I were deeply impressed by the fact that not only was she allowed to have a television in her bedroom, she was allowed to watch it *any time she wanted*. Only rarely were we permitted to watch with her—my mother knew for a fact that television destroyed brain cells—but she snuck us all into her room on the night Ed Sullivan introduced four boys from Liverpool. "Girls, come and see," she said, hustling us onto her bed and closing the door. *"You think you lost your love, Well I saw her yesterday-yi-yay . . ."* My grandmother's eyes were sparkling; her cigarette lay burning away in the ashtray. *"It's you she's thinkin' of . . ."* "My, my, *my*," she said, tapping her foot and bobbing her head no less vigorously than Willy does with his iPod, all these years later, "they sure are cute."

At eleven I still thought I hated boys, but my grandmother sure was right: they sure were cute. For days I went to school and did my homework and drifted off to sleep humming, *"Yeah, yeah, yeah."* At my next piano lesson I found myself thinking *"Yeah, yeah, yeah"* as I played the C-sharp major and minor scales. I wondered if Mrs. Witschey ever watched *The Ed Sullivan Show*. I wondered what she would have thought about the cute boys from Liverpool. I even went so far as to wonder how one would play the very last chord of the song—*"Yeah, yeah, yeah, **yeah**"*—on the piano; that chord had gotten to me at some level I had no way to comprehend. I finished my scales and looked over at Mrs. Witschey. "Let me hear the Haydn, dear," she said, opening my sonata book with those marble fingers of hers.

It occurs to me now that had I asked her about the chord,

she would probably have known exactly how to play it. Mrs. Witschey's background included not only a Juilliard education but a childhood in small-town West Virginia, filled with the music of county fairs and silent movie houses as well as piano recitals and church choirs. It's not impossible, in fact, that she found the boys from Liverpool as beguiling as my grandmother did. At the time, though, it seemed clear that "She Loves You" had no place in my piano lesson.

Popular music had no place, in fact, in any of my piano lessons. My teachers dwelt happily in the vast and magnificent world of classical music, and why not? Pop music, particularly rock and roll, represented the antithesis of the kind of artistic refinement and virtuosity to which they had devoted their careers. No wonder they pulled up the drawbridges. And whereas Mrs. Witschey and I never so much as broached the subject, some of my later teachers had emphatic things to say about rock and roll. "This stuff on the radio," said Madame Dmitrieff, who hailed from Russia, "I think it is the sound of hell."

"I can't listen to it," said Kay Bane, the delicate and tranquil young woman—even her name was tranquil—who succeeded Madame Dmitrieff as my teacher. "It hurts my ears," she added, covering them with her hands as though even the thought of that drumbeat was too loud.

It was not only my teachers who fended off the vulgar affront of pop. When I went to music camp as a teenager, I was astonished to find a storm brewing over popular music among the campers themselves. The front lines were commanded by David Finckel, son of the camp owner and a prodigiously gifted cellist (now widely known as a concert artist, member of the Emerson String Quartet and codirector of the Lincoln Center Chamber Music Society). David was committed to what we would call these days a zero-tolerance policy for rock music; he was certain that a more lenient approach would bring the camp down in ruins, with the entire world of classical music following shortly thereafter. I will not forget David's vocal disapproval the day he walked by my cabin as my bunkmates and I were listening to the transistor radio one of us had brought. What were we listening to? "Jumpin' Jack Flash," maybe, or "Sunshine of Your Love." Whatever it was, David considered it worse than transgression; like Madame Dmitrieff, he seemed to experience it as the devil's music. I had a tremendous crush on him, heightened of course by his passionate indignation; but as soon as he was gone, we turned the radio back on again. "*Hurry down to a stoned soul picnic,*" we sang along, very, very softly.

Am I dealing with the devil when I entertain pop music within the walls of my musical sanctum? Maybe, but the deal is done. There is nothing that makes Stephanie happier at the piano than that descending bass line: "*I look at you all, see the love there that's sleeping . . .*" There is nothing that absorbs

Susie's full attention as much as steering her painstaking way through the thirds of the teen lovers' chorus. And there is nothing, I'll admit, that I find more pleasurable than watching tiny Jenny breathe easier as she puts aside the arduous business of reading A, B and C, and traces, as if drawing it, the melody of "Dancing Queen" on the piano keys.

"Jenny, that's great," I say. "Maybe that's what you should play in the recital."

"Sure, if I play in the recital, which I'm not," says Jenny. There are times when a bit of mangled syntax means exactly, precisely what it says.

CHAPTER THREE

The Lure of *Elise*

*H*aving let loose the beast of popular music within the walls of my piano studio, here is what I discover, again and again: children love classical music.

Not all classical music, of course, and not all children. But many children—and surprising ones, sometimes. Kids whose parents, I am fairly sure, do not often listen to Beethoven or Chopin or Copland at home—kids who strike me as firmly rooted in the conventions and fashions of contemporary pop culture—will quite often express a preference bordering on longing for one or another piece of classical music.

There is for example Christopher, a soccer player with a mop of dark hair, whose parents own the town trattoria.

When Christopher begins lessons at the age of eight, one of the first pieces he masters is the beginner's version of the "Ode to Joy" in his lesson book. I tell him he plays it very well, which is true. "Can I play another song by Beethoven?" he asks immediately. "I just love his stuff."

The "song" he has in mind, he mentions, goes "Duh-duh-duh-DUH." So we embark upon the melody of the Fifth Symphony—why not? —until its melodic hairpin turns grow too difficult. A year or two later he has a new idea. "I wanna learn that thing by Mozart," he says. I wonder what he could possibly have heard by Mozart. I play him a bit of *Eine Kleine Nachtmusik*; he shakes his head no. Sonata in C? No. I hum the little tune that begins the *Turkish Rondo*. That, he says instantly, that's it, I want to play that. Christopher is not yet reading music fluently, so I teach him, by ear, a rudimentary version of the *Turkish Rondo*, one phrase per week. Every week he manages to remember his new phrase plus everything that went before; he goes home and practices on a tinny little electric keyboard. At the end of a year he can play about a minute and a half of music. When he plays it, his face is limpid with concentration. As soon as he has played the last note, he starts at the beginning again.

Where did Christopher first hear the *Turkish Rondo*? He heard it on television, of course. It is TV, ironically enough, that gives many kids their first and sometimes only exposure to classical music—usually as short sound bites in the soundtracks to movies, cartoons, commercials. Video games have become another source of exposure in recent years, although a classical melody reborn as the audio portion of a video game may not be anything its composer would recognize.

It's difficult to fathom the depth of the cultural change that has taken place since my childhood, when a Mother Goose–bedecked record player and an album of LPs heavy as dessert plates constituted a veritable treasure. It is even harder to imagine the musical world of my mother's generation, for whom records were almost iconic. When my mother was thirteen, a revered brother-in-law brought her a record of Tchaikovsky's Fourth Symphony. It was the first classical record she had ever seen. "I used to put it on the record player when I came home from school," she says, "and sit in my living room and listen to it." Try, if you will, to imagine a contemporary thirteen-year-old sitting alone and still in the late-afternoon light and listening—simply listening—to a symphony.

Even in our exponentially busier world, there are, of course, children who hear classical music at home. Max, at the age of fourteen, was inspired to spend a series of lessons constructing a piano version of the opening section of Beethoven's Fifth, the same symphony that had captivated Christopher. His parents had played the recording so often that he had whole sections of it in his head, and he slid back and forth along the piano bench rendering now the double bass part, now the flute line, with a fair degree of accuracy and immense athletic delight. (On the other hand, Max is also an example of how such culturally conscientious child-rearing can backfire; upon his fifteenth birthday he turned abruptly, systematically rebellious and refused to play any classical music at all.)

And there is the occasional child who has heard a memorable piece of classical music in school. Sadly, this is the exception rather than the rule. School music classes, apart from the occasional foray into *Peter and the Wolf*, tend to concentrate on keeping kids singing—an understandable choice, since when a kid is singing he cannot by definition be talking or yelling or fighting, and I know from experience that a school music teacher's overwhelming goal, every moment of every day, is to stave off chaos.

So a child who comes to me with a classical tune stuck in her head is most likely to have absorbed it from some facet of popular culture. "I heard it on that car commercial," she'll say, or "You know that ad for potato chips?" Sometimes children don't really know where they've heard what they've heard. They only know that it has stayed with them, and that they like it.

What they've heard, more often than anything else, is *Für Elise*. I cannot count the number of times a student has said to me, "I want to learn that song that goes 'Da-de da-de da-de da-de DA...'" And they learn it, all of them. They learn simplified versions, stretching tiny fingers across more keys than I would have believed they could. Or they learn the complicated version Beethoven actually wrote, slogging through the unfamiliar sections to get back to that irresistible "Da-de da-de da..." Or they learn intermediate and sometimes highly idiosyncratic versions. I'll admit that I groan inwardly at each new request—only to find that the child's deep and spontaneous pleasure allows me to experience yet again what it is to hear this music for the first time.

Many students, on the other hand, come to me with no classical music in their heads whatsoever. And some come quite confident that they hate classical music. There is Devon, for example, who counts on me never to forget just how deeply he hates it. Devon is thirteen, gangly, sweetly intractable; his mother loves Chopin, his father sings solos in church, his sister played Schumann when she studied with me. He will not, he informs me, play classical music. So for several years I have painstakingly steered Devon around the standard repertoire, mapping detours through ragtime, pop, jazz, rock. Devon particularly likes movie music and would be happy playing the soundtrack to *The Nightmare Before Christmas* for the rest of his life. But he is undeniably musical, and so in his fourth year of study I decide to sneak up on him. Without commentary or explanation, I present him with an intermediate-level piano arrangement of a Brahms

Hungarian Dance. He eyes the title and composer's name suspiciously. "It's part of some movie soundtrack, I think," I say, assuring my appalled conscience that, well, it certainly could have been, couldn't it? He learns the piece fairly quickly and plays it better than he has ever played anything, rendering the melodramatic tempo changes with tremendous flair. His parents and I discuss the issue of full disclosure. Shouldn't Devon be informed at some point that he is playing classical music? "Maybe you should tell him," I suggest.

"No, you can tell him," they assure me. You'd think we were preparing to tell Devon there is no Santa Claus.

Most of my students do not require such stratagems; they will muster a look of polite resignation when I assign them their first classical piece. I think of Margot, a teenager whose most enthusiastic achievements at the piano have been "Box of Rain" and "Sugar Magnolia." Margot's mother plays a red electric bass. Her father has had special shelving built into their basement to accommodate all his bootleg recordings of Grateful Dead concerts. "Margot, I would like you to try a Mozart sonata," I say. She greets this news with admirable composure. I choose the simple one in C major, the most famous sonata of all; she thinks she might have heard it someplace. The first few weeks feel like drudgery, and I am often tempted to stop, but then we get to the development section, where the left and right hands trade arpeggios in an unfolding ladder-like harmonic progression known as a circle of fifths. She comes to her lesson playing the arpeggios slowly but perfectly, using the damper pedal with unaccustomed clarity, and the transparent loveliness of that circle of fifths, intact across the centuries, is tangible in my studio. "I like it," says Margot, mystified.

Margot's younger sister Amy loves show tunes even more than she loves the Grateful Dead. When she comes upon a piece in her lesson book labeled "Sonatina," by someone named Duncombe who definitely did not write show tunes, she looks skeptical, to say the least. I encourage her to give it a try. There are all kinds of roadblocks: the left hand starts out in the treble clef; the right hand switches between triplet figures and eighth notes; the fingering of the sequence in the little bridge is confusing. Amy's expression changes from skepticism to dismay, and when her lesson ends, I am as convinced as she is that Duncombe's "Sonatina" is a lost cause. Later that week in the grocery store, Amy's mother asks me what the new song is. "She plays it constantly," she says, "she really likes it."

They like it. Often, they really like it. And I cannot help but wonder why. What is the allure of Dvořák or Beethoven or Mozart for kids who live by the insistent, pelvis-grinding beat of pop culture? What do they hear in classical music, and what does it mean to them? Why, finally, do they like it?

The simplest and most appealing answer, of course, is that beauty is inarguable. Philosophers have cherished this idea ever since Plato celebrated "beauty absolute, separate, simple and everlasting" and Plotinus described the principle of the beautiful as "something that is perceived at first glance, something which the soul names as from an ancient knowledge." Nearly two millennia later, Kant's view was not very different: "The beautiful is that which pleases universally without requiring a concept."

As a child listening to the well-worn records of my beloved collection, I never doubted the universal appeal of the beautiful. I was utterly certain that anyone who heard a Beethoven symphony or a Rachmaninoff concerto would feel as I did—breathless, ecstatic, almost afraid, as if engulfed and borne aloft by some majestic tidal wave. When I was eleven and living in West Virginia, my piano teacher Elizabeth Witschey—she of the beautiful white fingers and genteel diction—arranged for me to play a movement of Mozart's Piano Concerto in A Major with the local youth orchestra. A tidal wave it was not, but it was certainly beautiful, and I fell in love with it. One evening, as my father drove me home from a piano lesson with the sunset burning red behind the mountains, I explained to him that if everyone on earth could hear Mozart, there would never be another war. He nodded, as if this were only logical. "Music hath charms to soothe the savage breast," he said. Well, exactly. It was not until years later, when I learned the rest of the couplet—"To soften rocks, or bend a knotted oak"—that I realized my father hadn't made it up on the spot.

It is a lovely idea, this certainty of philosophers and children—lovely and, unfortunately, impossible to sustain; life in the modern world schools us in the cultural relativity of beauty. Plato and Kant may have found the principle of universality obvious in theory, but as a practical matter there's no denying that Beethoven's Fifth would be meaningless to someone who has heard nothing but, say, Arabic music all his life—or to someone in ancient Greece, for that matter.

For Amy and Christopher and Margot, though, pop-saturated as they are, the meanings and resonance of classical music seem to be surprisingly accessible. Perhaps it's not really so surprising. After all, the language of Western classical music is also the language of Western pop music. And by language I mean, in the most general sense, the harmonic system we call tonality.

Tonal music is by its very definition goal-oriented, and thus has a dimension of drama and suspense. The goal that orients a piece of music written in G major, for instance, is the note G and by extension the G-major chord (made up of G, B and D); we call this "goal" chord the tonic chord. All the other chords used in the piece will necessarily have a dramatic aspect to them, as they serve to move the music either toward or away from the tonic. The chord built atop the fifth note of the scale—that V chord, also called the dominant chord—takes us a short distance away but keeps us thinking of home; when this chord is enriched by the addition of an extra note—now it's called a dominant seventh chord—we are positively yearning to go home again. In contrast, the IV chord, called the subdominant, feels slightly further away; it stands at a certain contemplative distance from the tonic. And the chord built on the sixth scale note is the relative minor chord; it gives us a somber perspective on home. I tell my students sometimes that the dominant seventh chord is the doorstep of home, tilted moreover to make the return virtually inevitable; the subdominant chord is perhaps the grassy patch just beyond the doorstep, and the relative minor chord stands in the shadow of home. Harmonic and melodic dissonances introduce elements of conflict, moving the music further afield; consonances resolve the conflicts, and lead homeward.

We all know these meanings, these dramatic resonances, without ever having been taught them; we've been learning them unconsciously from the moment the overhead mobile went around and around playing "Twinkle, Twinkle, Little Star." We may never have heard of a subdominant chord or a dominant seventh; but simply by hearing music throughout our lives that is organized tonally, every one of us can experience the emotional and dramatic implications of these chords, and others, in relation to the "home" chord.

Popular music tends to use this language in a fairly simple way; its level of sophistication is, more often than not, about equivalent to that of "Twinkle, Twinkle." Dramatically and emotionally, therefore, it packs about the same punch. But the tonal drama is there—even if it's simple, and even if it's in the background, nearly buried by the beat. So it does the job of preparing Christopher and Devon to be able to hear classical music, to know how to listen for the fundamental elements of the drama—away from home, and home again; from repose through conflict to resolution—and to invest those elements with feeling.

Classical music, of course, commands a harmonic vocabulary that is vastly more sophisticated, and thus vastly more expressive. The G-major chord may still be home; but in the hands of a great classical composer, the journey away from home will be fraught with adventure and surprise, and the return, often lengthy and full of twists and turns, may be jubilant or reluctant or majestic. Often, both journeys will be limned with magnificent melodies and enlivened by sophisticated rhythmic patterns. In this music the drama of tonality is still understandable, but it takes on levels of emotional meaning that are richer, deeper, more mysterious and sublime. Children who are open to being moved—that is, most children—can hear and respond to these meanings.

Tanya, at thirteen, knows that she really likes the first movement of the *Moonlight* Sonata. She isn't sure why she likes it or where she heard it, but she is quite definite about wanting to play it. Tanya is Damian's older sister, and she has an iPod of her own, filled with what the radio stations call "hip-hop-and-R-and-B." She is tall and strong and, in my experience so far, considerably more interested in basketball than in the piano. I express concern that her music-reading skills might not be advanced enough to try something so long and so hard. She shrugs. "I could do it," she says. "I know how it's supposed to sound."

Tanya begins to learn the first movement of the *Moonlight* Sonata, in C-sharp minor. It is, in fact, far beyond her reading abilities; she has never played anything with more than one or two sharps in the key signature. I have to talk her, note by note, through every single measure. At the end of a month she can play two lines of music, haltingly and with mistakes.

"This isn't how it's supposed to sound," she says, acutely frustrated.

Maybe we should leave it for now, I suggest, and come back to it later, after she's had more practice at reading music? She shrugs. I know what that means.

On we go. More weeks go by. We make our laborious way through the third line, and the fourth. She negotiates the repeated dotted figure in the melody with excruciating difficulty. She learns bass clef notes she never saw before, forgets them, learns them again. She reads sharps as flats,

flats as sharps. Her tenacity and determination in the face of these hurdles is astonishing. But there is a point when she is, I can tell, ready to give up. And then we come to the measure where Beethoven arrives at B minor—only to shift on the third beat into B major, a shift that involves simply the change from a D natural to a D sharp. She plays that measure and stops. "Whoa," she says.

She has heard it, the way the plangent desolation of B minor is cracked open by that D sharp; she has felt the abrupt stab of joy, like an unearned blessing, of the move from minor to major. Whoa, indeed.

She spends the rest of the year learning the first movement of the *Moonlight* Sonata. At the end of the year she can play the whole thing by memory. Technically, she's in over her head; she plays very slowly, and she still makes mistakes here and there. But as the restless harmonies wash through key after key before finally coming to shore in the long, whispered, infinitely sad chords at the end, she is immersed in feeling.

Haley, also a teenager, knows she really likes Schubert's Impromptu in E-flat Major. More technically accomplished than Tanya, she is able to learn to play it fairly quickly. But like Tanya, she is not sure why the music exerts such a magnetic attraction for her. "It's weird," she says, "I never practice my other stuff anymore, I only practice this. I don't know why I like it so much."

I think I know why. Should I try to tell her? The Impromptu is a perfect example of how the simplest tonal events can be transmuted into a rich, complex and deeply moving dramatic arc. Here's what happens, I say to her, as though I'm telling a story. In the first section, a sunny waterfall of triplets in E-flat major, we move briefly away from the tonic chord, first to the dominant, then to the subdominant, and each time immediately back home. It's graceful, charming and entirely predictable, precisely the same harmonic scenario as, say, "Down by the Bay," or any of a thousand other well-known songs. The three-quarter time signature and the gentle rocking motion of the left hand give the harmonic to-and-fro a lithe, lighthearted dance feel.

In the next episode we hear the same charming little tale again, an octave higher. Then, after an interlude of wandering away through a circle of fifths, we are back home for yet a third repetition. Ah yes, we know this story, we think: home, away to the dominant, home again, away to the subdominant, home again . . .

And here, Haley, the plot thickens. An entirely unexpected move in the bass line, to D flat instead of D natural, turns the "home" chord into a new "doorstep" chord, shifting the identity of home. Upon which, immediately, the bass line steps down again—the new tonic is in turn upended and becomes a dominant leading to another tonic—and over and over this happens, the bass line moving relentlessly downward and teasing us toward a new home chord with every step. We are excited, dazzled, deeply unsettled, as the music moves us further and further away from the sunlit simplicity of the opening and lands finally in another territory altogether, a tempestuous middle section of shifting and darkening minor harmonies.

And then? And then, after an adventurous, rhythm-tossed sojourn in these stormy parts, we return at last to the E-flat waterfall, to the tranquil predictability of tonic-dominant-tonic, and we come, eventually, to rest at home. "It's beautiful," says Haley, and I can see that she is moved. Is it beautiful because it moves us, or does it move us because it's beautiful? In this music, as in all great art, beauty and feeling are fused.

Again and again, I see my students moved by the emotional eloquence of classical music. And it is fascinating to observe how different students respond to different elements of the tonal drama. For Clinton, a talented twelve-year-old, it is clearly the dark, spare beauty of minor keys that touches him. He's indifferent to anything in a major key, but he is brought up short by a Bach minuet in G minor. Pia, on the other hand—also talented and twelve—adores the effusive sweep of Chopin; she is stirred by the way the sinuous melodies evolve and mutate, accumulating lyrical flourishes here, heightened pauses there, so that what begins as pure melancholy ends in something like rapture. Penny, sweet and reserved, loves her sprightly little piece by Haydn.

Its rapidly shifting chords sometimes elude her fingers, but she is unmistakably happy whenever she plays it. As I listen to Clinton's brooding, elegiac rendition of his Bach minuet, or watch Penny's private smile at the final cadence of her Haydn *Allegro*, I am aware of knowing these children at a profound level—of glimpsing what might have been called, in a more old-fashioned time, their souls.

And of course I am baring my soul to them as well. As I guide my students through their pieces, exclaiming "Fortissimo!" here and "*Big* ritard" there, they come to know more and more precisely just what nuances of musical feeling excite and move me the most. There is a moment near the end of Debussy's *Clair de Lune*, for example, when the main theme, which outlines a D-flat-major chord, returns exactly as it was heard in the beginning . . . exactly, except for the addition of a single note, a C flat. The C flat has the effect of changing the D-flat chord into a D-flat dominant seventh chord—a gentle move away from the tonic chord that is, for me, particularly heartrending in its poignancy, a sudden ineffable sorrow in the heart of the chord. When I tell sixteen-year-old Chloe that this note might be the most important one in the piece, I feel almost as though I have told her a secret about me and I wonder if she can grasp it. She plays the passage again, hesitating before the chord and then sinking into it; there it is, that C flat, sad, surprising, inevitable. She knows the secret now, too.

I have a vivid memory of the first time I was aware of knowing a teacher in this way. The memory involves the fiery Madame Dmitrieff, whose devotion to classical music was as passionate as her disapproval of pop. I was twelve when I began lessons with Madame; my family had moved from West Virginia to Washington, D.C., and my mother had heard that Tamara Dmitrieff was one of the finest piano teachers in the area, as well as one of the most sought after. "I am taking no new students," said Madame Dmitrieff when my mother called. My mother never understood that sentence in relation to any of her three daughters, and in short order I was climbing the stairs to Madame's studio with a new book of Rachmaninoff preludes under my arm.

My hands were not really big enough yet for Rachmaninoff, but for Madame Dmitrieff, Rachmaninoff was a matter of heart. "Play deep!" she admonished as I worked my way through the splayed chords of the C-sharp-Minor Prelude. "Imagine the piano keys are a foot deep . . . go deep down, all the way down!" And when I came to the middle section, with its fierce chromatic melody and turbulent arpeggios: "More feeling! More feeling! You are playing gloom, okay, but you must play despair, you must play anguish!" I played with as much feeling as I could muster; I tried my twelve-year-old best to play anguish and despair. Mostly I was trying to get the notes right, but I can remember that as I played, the phrase "the Russian soul" came into my mind, and I thought I understood it.

I did not know then what I learned years later: that Madame Dmitrieff had been the daughter of a palace guard at the court of Czar Nicholas II, that as a child she had studied with Rachmaninoff himself, and that her family had been forced to flee the country and live in exile when the czar was overthrown. Even without knowing these things, though, I was aware that the brooding sadness of this music had a deeply personal meaning for Madame. In time, of course, my hands were able to grasp those chords and negotiate those arpeggios more easily, and Rachmaninoff's journey through despair took on its own shades of meaning for me. I never forgot, though, the moment when even with smaller hands, I grasped something essential about Madame Dmitrieff. And when I talk Margot through her Mozart sonata—pointing out the brilliant effect of the arrival at a new key at the end of the exposition, exclaiming over the harmonic and melodic gymnastics of the development, delighting in the sly cadence that tricks us into thinking we are "home" in C again, only to launch into further harmonic hikes—I know that Margot knows some essential things about me. Can she handle it?

She can, it seems. Most students can. On occasion, though, a child will find the intensity of feeling unmanageable. There was, unforgettably, the time that little Rosie seemed to be spellbound, leaning toward me as I explained the dramatic tension inherent in a suspension chord and the relief and delight of its resolution. "Do you understand what I mean?" I said, gratified by her rapt attention. She leaned closer. "Oh my God," she said, "where did you get your earrings?"

I realized it was simply too much—too much suspense, too much resolution, too much intensity of feeling. I decided, not without regret, that suspension chords would have to wait for another day, another year. "Macy's," I said.

....

IT HAS BEEN FASHIONABLE for many years now to lament the impending death of classical music in modern culture. "Classical music has seemingly ceased to exist in American society," pronounced a music critic in the *New York Times* ten years ago. Only last year another *Times* critic asked his readers, "Is the business of classical music, as we know it, dying?" Performers, managers, recording industry executives, cultural commentators—all are perennially worried that classical music is about to fall suddenly, permanently silent in the face of the relentless and unstoppable roar of mainstream pop.

It was this apprehension, I think, that motivated David Finckel at music camp to denounce the insidious lure of the Rolling Stones and the Grateful Dead. David's father, Ed

Finckel, the camp director and a well-known and much-loved musician, was considerably more sanguine than his son about the prospects of classical music; throughout a long career as a school music teacher, a choral director and a jazz player in the days when jazz was cool and hot and glamorous and disreputable all at once, he remained convinced that great works of musical art would endure. David was less certain; I think he feared that if pop music gained a foothold, the Dead would inevitably trounce Dvořák in winning the hearts and minds of campers.

David, already a virtuosic cellist at the age of seventeen, was working on the Dvořák cello concerto that summer, and asked me to play the piano reduction of the orchestra part with him. When I wrapped my hands around those smoldering chords as he ignited the melody line . . . well, it was the sexiest music on earth. What on earth, I wondered, was he worried about?

Music camp was, in fact, the place where I discovered the varieties of romantic and erotic passion that can be evoked by classical music. And I was not alone. We were adolescents, after all. We may have played "Sugar Magnolia" now and then in our cabins, but in the dining hall at lunchtime we put the Brahms Double Concerto on the record player and nearly swooned over our peanut butter sandwiches. When the camp orchestra played the Fourth Brandenburg Concerto, the string sections hummed voluptuously along as the young soloists on flute and violin engaged in a mad musical flirtation. And there was the night we gathered around the camp's one little black and white TV to watch Neil Armstrong walk on the moon, and then played Beethoven's *Fidelio* Overture on the dining hall record player; there was simply no other way to express the amazement and wonder we all felt. Then we went skinny-dipping in the wide swath of light thrown across our lake by that very moon. Space travel, Beethoven, nudity; the connections felt obvious. David could rest easy. Classical music was, for every one of us aspiring musicians, charged with all kinds of power—amorous, erotic, creative, spiritual—at a level that rock music could never hope to approach.

Undeniably, pop music can be seductive. But I have never seen its appeal turn a child against classical music. I think of Haley, the teenager who succumbed to the spell of the Schubert Impromptu. Haley had come to me initially at the age of fourteen, having left a teacher who had rigorously schooled her in piano classics for a number of years. "I hear you let kids play fun stuff sometimes," she said to me at our first lesson. I let her play some fun stuff: Broadway showstoppers, hip-hop riffs, contemporary pop. She played all this music with gusto; she was clearly having fun. And after about a year she came to a lesson with her old collection of piano classics sandwiched between "All That Jazz" and "Accidentally in Love." We started the Chopin Waltz in A

Minor, the one with the bleak and lovely melody in the left hand, and after a few more weeks I did not see "All That Jazz" again. Broadway may be alluring; Chopin is, in the end, irresistible.

It's interesting that the people in charge of marketing classical music don't seem to understand this. Symphony orchestras in particular have gone into a defensive tailspin. Rather than deploring the siren song of popular music, they seem to have decided to try to make classical music feel like pop. They offer preconcert get-togethers, video projections during performances, free T-shirts, even postconcert dance parties with DJs. They advertise Beethoven's Fifth as the *Star Wars* of symphonic music and Beethoven himself as the Kurt Cobain of his generation. They launch ad campaigns to the under-forty demographic that make a classical concert sound like a singles bar.

Is all this really necessary? I don't think so. If Chloe can hear Debussy, if Tanya can hear Beethoven and Haley can hear Chopin without any video projections or T-shirts, I think we can trust in the power of the music itself to move those whose spirits are open to being moved. As long as we have the emotional capacity to experience profound feeling, we will respond to classical music.

It's an interesting and relatively modern phenomenon, the split in our culture between classical and pop, art music and commercial music—and by "modern" I mean the last six hundred or so years. Before the increasingly sophisticated vocal music of the late Middle Ages made the development of music notation necessary, there was no art music in Western culture at all; there couldn't have been, since art music, almost by definition, is complex enough that it needs to be written down. Early medieval and ancient worlds enjoyed a wealth and variety of music, no doubt; but it had to be simple enough to be created, played and passed along by ear. All music, then, was popular music.

But as art music evolved and was nurtured first by the Catholic Church and then by the aristocracy, it became increasingly distinct from folk traditions. It's true that the classical music of nineteenth-century Europe broadened its appeal to large sections of the middle class, and Verdi's public awaited his every opera with the same feverish anticipation that contemporary America reserves for, say, the next U2 tour. But that was a fairly brief historical moment. In contemporary Western culture, the split between classical and popular has widened and intensified as the recording and entertainment industries have found in pop music a highly profitable commodity. It's much easier to mass-market "Sugar, Sugar" than a Beethoven symphony or even, for that matter, a Verdi opera. And so we're stuck with the split.

The doomsayers' fears are not without cause. It's true that classical music will never attract the mass audience that popular music enjoys. It's true, too, that popular music at its worst can be antithetical to the experience of beauty or authentic feeling. It can narcotize feeling and dull sensibility; it can stimulate without resonating, satiate without satisfying.

But consider the following quotation on the subject of contemporary music: "Our music today with its lasciviousness corrupts and contaminates." An eloquent paraphrase, certainly, of the convictions of David at music camp ... except that it was written in 1572 by a Florentine scholar named Vincenzo Galilei, father of the astronomer. Galilei was a member of the Renaissance intellectual circle the Camerata, whose guiding lights were appalled by the way the music of the younger generation was perverting the standards and morals of civilized society. A letter written to Galilei by a Roman scholar, Girolamo Mei, concurs with him that this music "doesn't try to penetrate the soul with an idea" or "to stir in someone an affection." He complains that it's dominated by "so much fear of boring the ear," and goes on to deplore "the disordered perturbation, mix-up and mangling of the words."

Interesting. Didn't your parents say something very similar about the Rolling Stones? And haven't you said it yourself, about the Smashing Pumpkins or 50 Cent?

The Renaissance humanists were certain that music's capacity to titillate, divert and distract would prove so seductive that its power to move the soul would be lost. Western musical culture proceeded, of course, to produce Bach, Mozart, Beethoven, Brahms, Ravel and Messaien as well as Green Day and the Red Hot Chili Peppers. All was not lost.

Even today, I believe, all is not lost. Classical music is still the most eloquent and compelling manifestation of the musical language we all know. It's harder than one might fear to subdue the human hunger for beauty, deep feeling and passionate expressiveness.

For pianists in particular, all is far from lost. Classical music and the piano are made for each other: the piano evolved to meet the developing expressive imperatives of classical composers, and the music itself, in turn, evolved along with the technical capacities of the instrument. Certainly, the piano can be a wonderful medium for other kinds of music as well. But play a work from the classical piano repertoire on a good piano, and you cannot help but know that the voice of the piano is inseparable from the heart and soul of the music.

It is my piano students, finally, who have convinced me of the enduring power of classical music. It's impossible to witness Clinton playing his Bach minuet or Pia playing her Chopin waltz without understanding that, for them, this music has vitality and spiritual force. Clinton and Pia, of course, are fairly accomplished students. Sometimes I find it even more compelling to witness the appeal of classical music to students for whom the technical struggle is especially great.

Consider Debbie, my Ben Folds Five aficionado. Debbie has played very little classical music but is a passionate follower of the brainier, more sophisticated pop singers on the contemporary scene; I help her learn to play this music by ear, and she plays it well and with deep satisfaction. And then Debbie brings me a classical CD her grandmother has given her. "Can I learn to play this?" she says, "I really like it."

To my considerable surprise, it is a Shostakovich piano concerto. My local music store has to order it from Russia. Debbie and I focus on the second movement, technically the most accessible. The music is full of dark, rich chords and austere modal melodies. Debbie loves it, and works on it peacefully for months. Clearly, her years with pop crooners have not rendered her tone deaf to the somber beauty of Shostakovich. The music does not come easily to her, and she struggles with many passages, but she doesn't tire of it. For her it is not a piece to master so much as a place to dwell.

Consider, more dramatically, Pablo, nineteen years old and six feet four inches tall and Hispanic, a guitar player in a Beatles tribute band who has decided he needs to learn to play the piano. I've seen a video of his band performing "Twist and Shout" at a festival. Pablo could not look less like John Lennon, but when he wails away on his guitar in a Carnaby Street black suit and sings *"Well, shake it up BA-by, now, shake it up, baby,"* I suspend disbelief.

I have to overcome a different sort of disbelief when I see Pablo at a piano. His fingers are so long that it is virtually impossible for him to play two adjacent keys; his thumbs seem to maintain an existence independent of the rest of his hands. He approaches the piano keyboard as though it's a sort of telegraph machine, poking at the keys with sticklike fingers. I manage to teach him a frenetic version of "Eleanor Rigby" and find myself secretly hoping that will be that. Not so fast: Pablo wants to learn Mozart. He hums the tune of the Sonata in C at me, the same sonata that took Margot by surprise. I find him a copy of the music and he goes to work. He never learns very much of it—Pablo will probably never play a great deal of Mozart—but what strikes me is that Pablo *hears* Mozart. It might seem a long way from the pure lucidity of the Sonata in C to "C'mon, c'mon, c'mon, c'mon, BA-by, now," but for Pablo there seems to be no distance at all. He masters the first eight measures and plays them again and again, smiling. "I love it," he says. "I don't know why."

Who knows why, exactly, Pablo responds to the beauty in a matched pair of Mozart phrases? Have the Beatles paved the way? Does Mozart evoke something from his childhood? Or is it something more abstract, some natural affinity he has for these bright, clear sonorities, for the graceful arcs of these tunes? Whatever the reason, Pablo has found in Mozart "something the soul names as from an ancient language."

Let us finally consider Damian, whose shiny new iPod is so proudly filled with hip-hop. Having spent the better part of a year alternating between the sprightly songs in his lesson book and the throbbing bass lines of the radio station "Hot 97," I ask Damian what he would like to prepare to play in the June recital. *Für Elise*, he replies without hesitation. "I love that song. I heard it on TV."

CHAPTER FOUR

Emerging

A friend and colleague of mine says, "I love the little ones." She finds her deepest delight as a piano teacher in the very first stages of learning: finding middle C, memorizing the names of the white keys, making the acquaintance of the musical staff. This is the time when each small step is big; a child can leave a piano lesson knowing conspicuously more than he did when he came. After a year or two, progress becomes slower, more incremental, more complicated. At this point my friend is happy to pass the student along to someone else and begin again from scratch with a new little one.

Other teachers I know prefer the budding virtuosi whom they can guide along the path to Interlochen or Juilliard. The charms of innocence leave them cold, but they are perennially energized by an ambitious, motivated young dynamo, a technically challenging passage, a sophisticated question of musical interpretation.

I can appreciate both points of view. But I also find something uniquely interesting and stimulating about the long, layered stage in between, that protracted and tricky passage from novitiate to expert. Progress happens slowly here, often so slowly as to be undetectable for long stretches of time. This is the stage when musical identities begin to emerge. It's the stage when kids are finding their particular strengths, their affinities, their challenges. And often, of course, it's the stage when kids quit.

Because it's hard, playing the piano, and it continues to get harder. As a student moves beyond the beginning stages, the issue of technique begins to loom large: developing proper hand and finger position, acquiring strength and independence of fingers, cultivating muscle control. An instrumentalist is an athlete. There is no way around the need for intense physical training; without it, the ability to play a Beethoven sonata is about as unlikely as the ability to pole-vault. But while pole-vaulters and soccer players and gymnasts usually practice together, a piano student practices his technical exercises alone, and it can feel like drudgery.

The book of finger exercises I use most frequently in my teaching was written in the nineteenth century by a fellow named Charles-Louis Hanon. The front of the exercise book, in its modern incarnation, is decorated with a sprightly painting by Matisse; on the first page is a message from Charles-Louis himself, guaranteeing that with the regular practice of these exercises "the fingers attain an astonishing facility," and further promising that the practitioner will "never again experience any stiffness or technical problems." Amazingly, my students usually manage to resist both the decorative allure of Monsieur Matisse and the snake-oil blandishments of Monsieur Hanon.

"I lost it," says Max.

"I forgot it," says Sara.

"My cleaning lady took it," says Matthew.

What can I say? I can preach the value of diligent labor and delayed gratification, but I am not likely to arouse much enthusiasm with this pitch. It occurs to me to wonder whether Matthew's cleaning lady would like piano lessons.

"You know," I say eventually, "it's like brushing your teeth. You just have to do it."

There are, of course, students who practice their Hanon without complaint, and now and then the student comes along who actually likes it. I think of Mark, a middle-schooler with an exceptionally methodical turn of mind. Mark has decided that he will play each Hanon exercise in three different keys. One week he plays the first exercise in C, C sharp and D; the following week he practices the second exercise in D sharp, E and F; after four weeks he has covered the twelve major keys and begins again with Exercise number 5 in C, C sharp and D. I am careful not to let Mark in on the fact that most of my students would consider this a particularly acute form of torture.

"You know, Mark," I say, "there are actually twelve more keys you could use—the minor keys."

"Cool," says Mark.

"And there are actually three different kinds of minor scales—"

"Thirty-six more," says Mark, "*yesss.*" Even his grin is methodical.

I don't think I ever relished playing technical exercises the way Mark does. But I don't remember hating them, either. The exercises I recall most vividly are not those of Hanon but a volume of technical studies by Carl Czerny. Czerny's exercises were actual compositions, lavish cascades of sixteenth notes that went on for pages and pages and were intended to perfect this or that aspect of one's technique. Madame Dmitrieff would watch my hands intently as I played them, alert to every nuance of finger and hand position. And when she was satisfied with my technique, she would exclaim, "Play it with feeling!"

My only feeling about Czerny's sixteenth notes was that I wanted to be finished with them as quickly as possible. "I thought it was just an exercise," I told her.

"And why can't you play an exercise with feeling?" she

retorted, and she sat on the bench beside me and proceeded to play my Czerny exercise with both technical perfection and a highly wrought expressiveness. I decided as I listened that Czerny must have been Russian, and that maybe he even knew Madame Dmitrieff.

I never did manage to invest Czerny with feeling. But there was something comforting about the specificity and exactness of the enterprise. I tried to visualize Madame Dmitrieff's strong, supple hands as I practiced, and I did my best to imitate the way they looked on the keys. Besides, it was like brushing my teeth: I just had to do it.

Every student who moves to the intermediate stage has to practice exercises. And every one of them has to practice scales—both to improve technical skills and to develop familiarity with the different keys. Scales, I have found, can incite the same kind of vigorous loathing as exercises. "Do I *have* to?"... "I did it *last* week"... "I forget the fingering..."

I actually enjoy playing scales, but I know what they're talking about. To play a major scale with both hands at the same time is a maneuver somewhere between a crossword puzzle and the last round of hopscotch. Here, for example, is what there is to think about when you are playing, say, two octaves of an A-major scale with both hands: *White note white note third note is C sharp right thumb under on D white note white note left third over on F sharp then G sharp right thumb under on A then left fourth finger over on B then C sharp right away right thumb under on D white note white note left third over on F sharp then G sharp A.*

And that only gets you halfway through the scale; you still have to come down again.

Just as some kids actually like exercises, though, some kids actually like scales. They like the Twister-like quality of the fingering; more, they like the deep sense of organization represented by a scale, which after all is a predetermined pattern of whole steps and half steps. And I like the fact that when students practice scales they are becoming familiar with the roadmaps of all twenty-four major and minor keys, those miniature dominions of hierarchy and order wherein lie all of tonality's profound capacities for beauty. Besides, it's great for their fingers.

Technique is more than fingers, of course; it's back and arms and shoulders, legs and feet. I think my first realization of this came at the age of eleven as I watched the gracious Mrs. Witschey sit down to demonstrate some point of technique or execution. She looked so elegant—her posture impeccable, her arms relaxed but poised, her chin with a slight tilt—that for many years she remained my image of how one should look when playing the piano. In this image she is wearing a white linen skirt, and a silk blouse and pearls. Perhaps I added the pearls as the years went by. But even without them, the image convinced me—and convinces me still—of the compatibility of ladylike elegance and technical power.

There are a number of truisms about the correct way to sit at the piano: back straight, shoulders down, elbows slightly out, arms aligned with wrists—you know the look. Students need to be pestered about all this at the same time they are busy learning correct finger technique. I find, though, that I need to be careful: there are times when a student's unorthodox physical tendencies are the ones that serve him best—and may be, in fact, the only way he can play the piano at all. In such cases, of course, truisms be damned. Consider Devon, the student I bamboozled into playing Brahms (who not only survived the experience but went on to play Schumann, even as his sister had before him). Devon at the age of fourteen is utterly akimbo—legs, arms, even hair—and alternates between two modes of being, somnolent and manic, sometimes more than once a minute. If I ask him to sit up straight and line up his feet one beside the other, he is practically immobilized, but when I allow him to slouch a little and stick his left leg out to the side, he can produce a rather spirited rendition of *The Wild Rider*—against all odds, from the look of it. While I don't encourage my students to emulate the famous Glenn Gould slump, I have discovered that the "right" way to sit at the piano is not exactly the same for any two children. The challenge is to distinguish between when an idiosyncrasy will serve the student and when it will get in his way. Susie may like to cross her legs when she plays, as if she is at a tea party; but it throws her off, and besides, she can't use the damper pedal that way. Devon, on the other hand, seems to gain a sense of balance from that lumberjack-style out-stretched leg. Lumberjack, yes; tea party, no. Piano teaching, in the intermediate stage, is made of such distinctions.

One of the most important technical challenges of this stage, in fact, is learning the correct way to use the damper pedal—the one on the right, which lifts all the dampers off the piano strings so that they can continue to vibrate and produce sound. There is a highly counterintuitive aspect to the coordination of hand and foot; with every downbeat, the foot must come very briefly up as the fingers come down. Some kids master this fairly easily, but others struggle; the foot comes up with the hand, which makes the sound choppy and disjointed, or it doesn't come up at all, which produces sludge. Then there is Pia, whose timing with the pedal is im-peccable but whose physical technique is problematic: in-stead of keeping her heel on the floor and using the upper part of her foot to press and release the pedal, she keeps her heel up and pedals with her entire foot, precisely as though she's operating one of those little hydraulic lifts with which you raise your car when you need to change a tire. Even when her playing sounds lovely, it can be tough to watch. "Pia, put your heel down," I say to her a dozen times a lesson. Pia has the talent to become a professional musician if she chooses—unless potential employers just can't get around that hyperactive hydraulic lift.

Perhaps the most obvious task of the intermediate stage is acquiring the ability to read music: it happens now, or most probably it will never happen. In the beginning stages, the task of reading music is something like deciphering a code. "All Cows Eat Grass," we chant as we point to the four spaces between the staff lines of the bass clef, where the notes A, C, E and G are written. For the five staff lines of the treble clef, I sometimes use the old-fashioned mnemonic "Every Good Boy Deserves Fudge," despite its aura of political and even nutritional incorrectness; in recent years some of my students have offered "Even George Bush Drives Fast" as an alternative, but I am fairly sure this does not represent any kind of advance in political consciousness. Using such little mantras to identify notes is not really reading music, though it's a necessary first step. To take the next step, the student has to move from cracking a code to understanding a language.

Which is, of course, hard. It takes time and practice and a great deal of patience. Having a knack for it doesn't hurt, either. Interestingly, this particular knack is not always connected with musicality; sometimes, in fact, the two are almost opposed. Every music teacher knows that musically talented children are liable to put off learning to read music, since they can simply reproduce what they hear. Pia came to me for lessons as an intensely gifted intermediate-level student, and it was quite a while before I caught on to the fact that she had a fairly dim idea of how to read music—was oblivious even to cows, grass, boys, fudge. "Would you just play it for me once?" she'd say whenever I introduced a new piece. Stupidly, I would, and she'd proceed to sit down afterward and play it back to me—melody, harmony, inner voicings, the works. With an ear that good, it was hard for Pia to buckle down to the tedious business of learning to read music; she is learning, but every now and then she tries again: "Would you just play that once . . . ?"

I have had a few students for whom reading music was such torture—for varying reasons—that at some point along the way they simply stopped, and learned everything by ear. I don't agree easily to this kind of arrangement, but there are times when it seems justified. Willy, for example, after years of lessons, still feels acute discomfort at the sight of written notes. No matter how many times I declaim slowly and clearly that in the bass clef, A is the note in the bottom space, Willy continues to greet the note in the bottom space with a blank expression just this side of panic. "Willy, what did I just tell you about the note in the bottom space?" I can say, and he will stare at the note, stricken, prayerful, for an entire minute, but he will not know. I have recently begun teaching Willy simple blues patterns, and Willy can play through twenty or thirty choruses without realizing he is practicing. "Tritones are so cool," says Willy with relief.

Tara, on the other hand, can read notes perfectly well if she wants to, but at the age of fourteen she decides she does not want to. Tara is a reserved, soft-spoken, delicate-looking girl, but when she says no, she means no. She is softly, delicately implacable on the subject for several years, during which time she devotes herself to learning by ear a number of the classic pop tunes she loves—not only Joni Mitchell's "Blue," but also songs by the Grateful Dead, Bob Dylan, Eric Clapton. (Need I even mention "Stairway to Heaven"?) And when she begins her senior year of high school, she decides, with the same kind of genteel determination, to start reading music again, and is thrilled by the world of music that opens up to her. It's just not feasible to learn Debussy by ear.

At the other extreme from Willy and Tara are the kids who take easily to reading music and are resistant to playing without notes in front of them. I cannot always predict which kids these will be; who would have thought, for example, that Devon, he of the gangly slouch, would refuse to play without written notes? One would assume, to look at him, that he'd prefer the looseness of playing by ear to the exactitude demanded by musical notation, but Devon will not relinquish the written page. "Maybe next week," he says, expressionless, whenever I suggest it. Perhaps the authority of those lines and spaces, notes and rests, helps Devon stave off chaos. "Devon has a very good ear," says his father, the church choir soloist. "Why don't you learn a blues or something, Dev?"

"Maybe next week," says Devon.

In general, kids who read books early and easily learn to read music easily. In general, girls learn to read music somewhat more easily than boys. And in general, learning to read music is an outstanding accomplishment. A good deal of time and energy is spent during the "emerging" years on this great task. When a student succeeds in learning to read music fluently, I know I have given her access to experiencing the beauty and richness of the whole world of music in a very powerful way.

Even so, I worry—just as I do with my beginners—about what may be lost. In life, of course, a substantial gain almost always involves loss of some kind, and piano lessons are no different. For one thing, it can be harder to learn what music is made of, if one plays mostly by reading. When I am teaching Tara to play "Layla" by ear, it's almost inevitable that we will investigate the harmony and structure of the song as she learns it. If she learned by reading the printed sheet music, on the other hand, she could easily perfect it without ever even considering those aspects of the song.

I know, because I learned music that way for a very long time. I became a handy sight-reader at an early age and loved nothing more than to ramble through miles of Mozart, relishing the beauty of the music and the feel of it in my hands without really thinking about much of anything at all. When I was fourteen and living in New York's Westchester County, though, the calm and mild-mannered Kay Bane decided it was time I started to understand the music I was playing. A green and white workbook called *Music Theory* appeared, and I was assigned several pages a week. I protested to my mother, not calmly, that these were supposed to be piano lessons, not math classes, but Mrs. Bane proved as strong-willed as she was mild-mannered; she prevailed, and I began to learn what music was made of. And whenever a student gets the hang of reading music so well that she begins to chew her way, eager but clueless, through sarabande after gavotte, I wonder whether that green and white workbook is still in print.

More profound than the potential loss of musical understanding, though, is the business of musical creativity—that starling on the windowsill whose primitive, untutored song is gradually lost to children as they learn conventional speech. And I can't get around the fact that the more successful I am in teaching a child to read music, the more likely it is that some part of her musical spontaneity will be lost, or at least buried.

By musical spontaneity I mean the capacity for making things up—for discovering sounds one enjoys, and playing with them. This has very little to do with art; the capacity to invent music that is both original and artistically meaningful is a rare gift. For most people, even musically inclined people, the sounds they make up are not "art," but are simply self-expressive—just as the sentences most people speak and write are not literary art but simply vehicles for expression and communication. Still, it's a lovely thing to express one-self through musical invention and play.

I have a vivid memory of Eddie at the age of thirteen, learning the definition of a minor chord. He was at that point still struggling to read music but was adept at playing scales, and when we got around to learning the minor scales, I explained that a minor chord uses steps 1, 3 and 5 of the scale. Eddie played an A-minor chord and held onto it as though it were telling him something. Then he played the notes of the chord separately, lowest to highest, highest to lowest. He had never given a major chord a second thought, but clearly this was something else. We proceeded to figure out the notes of a G-minor chord, then F minor, E minor. At his next lesson he played me an original composition built of a number of minor chords in succession, using a little arpeggiated pattern Philip Glass would not have been ashamed of. We named it, to Eddie's intense satisfaction, *Minor Chord Fantasia*.

I have never seen a student enjoy an original piece more than Eddie loved that composition. He played it at the beginning and end of every lesson. He played it, by his own admission and his parents' testimony, twenty or thirty times a day. It might not have been art, but it was Eddie's free play with a sound that excited and moved him. For Eddie, what art could be more valuable than that? I told him that I looked forward to further compositional ventures on his part, and he seemed to like that idea.

And then there was a complicating development. Christmastime came, and someone gave Eddie a big book of Christmas songs arranged for intermediate piano. It happens that Eddie is passionately fond of Christmas and of Christmas music. He dove headfirst into that big book and spent his holiday playing through the songs. At our first January lesson I discovered that Eddie, in one fell swoop, had learned to read music. Eureka, of course. But when I asked him to play his fantasia, he shrugged. "I kind of forgot it," he said.

It wasn't the first time I had seen this happen, and it would not be the last. I remember Matthew noodling on the black notes one day when the song on the page in front of him proved particularly impenetrable. His fingers happened upon a catchy, spiky fragment of melody that caught his attention; he played it again and then again. "Listen," he said, "look what I got," as if he had caught a fish. Once the difficult page of notes was deciphered, though, the fish got away; he couldn't remember the melody he had invented, and was visibly bored when I played it for him.

And I remember Clinton, who not only composed a bluesy little piece but wrote it painstakingly down and brought it to a lesson. Clinton, normally reserved and often self-critical, managed to feel very proud of that piece. But by the time recital season came and I asked him if he would perform it, he had improved his music-reading skills to the extent that he found his own composition embarrassing.

Eddie and Matthew and Clinton are still taking piano lessons and are developing into highly creative interpretive musicians. But the authority of the printed page has somehow undermined their impulse to make things up. They may not consciously miss the spiky melody, the hand-penciled notes, the fantasia—but I do. And I hope that at some point they can manage to get past their hard-won comfort with reading notes, and find their various ways back, at least now and then, to spontaneous musical utterance.

I know that this can in fact happen—at any age—because it happened for me at the unlikely age of forty-seven, when I was asked to play keyboard in a local blues band. "I don't play keyboard," I said. "And I don't play blues."

"It's not hard," I was assured. "You'll pick it up in no time."

I picked it up, although it took me some time. I got myself a keyboard and I learned a few ways to play the three chords of the twelve-bar blues pattern; grinding out those thick blues chords was as satisfying as kneading dough. But when it came time during a rehearsal for me to play a solo, I froze. It had been many, many years and thousands of pages of music ago that I had perched on a piano bench and come up with *In the Moonlight*. I couldn't locate in myself even the slightest impulse toward spontaneous improvisation.

I decided that someone else's improvisation would have to do. I listened over and over to an album of Pinetop Perkins, one of the great inventors of blues piano, and figured out how to play a few of his bluesy licks. The next time I was called upon to solo, I simply played a few of Pinetop's licks end to end. I was not showered with accolades, but I wasn't drummed out of the band, either, and my paralysis gradually abated.

As time went on, I began to break up my canned solo with brief interludes of spontaneous improvisation. At every performance my pulse would race and my palms sweat, and I was vastly relieved when it was over. I never, ever became fluent. Once in a while, I stumbled upon a few notes that did not sound like Pinetop Perkins or Eric Clapton or B.B. King—that sounded, I supposed, like me. But it always felt like walking out on the wing of an airplane.

And there's no denying it: as my students learn to read music, they tend to be less and less inclined to try that walk. Most do not even think of trying. So I remind them now and then, and try to administer a gentle shove out onto the wing whenever I think they might be receptive.

There was the time, for example, when Pia was deeply engaged in trying to distract me from discovering that she had practiced none of the pieces I had assigned her that week. "I made something up," she said, with calculated charm, "want to hear it?" She began to play a slapdash series of bright and furiously arpeggiated chords, hands flying, brow furrowed, right leg pumping hard as she went after that hydraulic pedal.

I knew she was making it up on the spot, buying time, but I liked it. "It's great, Pia," I said, "keep your heel on the floor. And by next week I want you to create a complete piece from that idea, with a beginning, middle and end." Which meant, of course, another week without Chopin and Beethoven, but the result was worth it; she came to the next lesson with a lively little composition.

"I can't think of a name for it," she said, stalling for more time.

"It sounds like sunlight to me," I offered.

In a changing world, Pia's strong objection to being controlled is wonderfully constant. "It does *not*," she said. "In fact, I just decided what it's called—it's called *Lullaby for the Moon*."

Sometimes a composition starts with a mistake, an accidental wrong note or chord that catches the student's fancy; I correct the mistake, but the student is reluctant to part with it. "Ella, that C chord should not have an F sharp in it," I say when Ella reaches the final measure of *The Entertainer.*

She is startled; she plays the chord again, complete with the F sharp. "I *like* it there," she declares.

"But it doesn't really sound like an ending, does it?"

"So maybe it's *not* the ending."

Aha! The airplane wing. "Okay," I say casually, "so what might come after it?" She plays the bristly chord once more, thinking; then she plays another, bristlier still. "Keep going," I say, and bless her, she does, producing a series of excruciating chords Schoenberg would have been proud of.

I remember a student improvising a *Dance of the Butterflies*; another student composing a stern *Midnight March*; and another who at every lesson embellished upon his musical melodrama *The Monkey and the Gorilla*. All of these arose from some chance circumstance, whether a willful mistake, a diversionary tactic, or something as simple as an unbidden impulse. I felt pleased, in each case, that I had been able to help a student retrieve his or her capacity for musical invention.

I'm much less successful, though, when it comes to the one musical genre that actually requires improvisation. I refer, of course, to jazz.

My sons and I learned to love jazz from their father, a virtuosic jazz musician. Adam, our older son, went to sleep every night between the ages of six and ten or so listening to

Ben Webster; his younger brother Evan demanded Dizzy Gillespie and Charlie Parker at bedtime for years. (Marvelously, "Salt Peanuts" put him right to sleep, something like the way too much chocolate cake can induce coma.) Both have taken many more lessons on the saxophone than on the piano, yet their fingers meet the piano keys easily, automatically, in the shapes of jazz voicings and sonorities. I don't understand this—who can fully understand how her children know what they know?—but I find it a constant source of amazement and delight. Over the years, my sons—Evan on the saxophone accompanied by Adam at the piano—have provided me with a rich informal education in the great standards of the jazz repertoire.

But although I love to listen to jazz, I can't play it. My hands simply don't find their way to those jazz chords that are in my sons' bones. And while I can occasionally fake a blues solo, there's no faking a jazz solo. So I can't teach jazz.

This has proven problematic only occasionally; when my piano students say they want to learn to play jazz, they usually have *The Pink Panther* in mind, or the theme from *Mission: Impossible*. I can teach them these immortal works, of course, and we can proceed to work our way through a collection or two of jazzy-sounding pieces for intermediate piano. For most students, that's enough; not many really want to solo on the changes of "Maiden Voyage." Jazz is a musical language unfamiliar to this generation—and it's deeply, dauntingly hard. But a few persist. And when they do, I can take them only so far.

Clinton is one who has persisted. One of my most clearly talented students, he has a fair amount of technical skill and plays classical music well and willingly—as long as it is in a minor key, of course—but his love for jazz is passionate to the point of ferocity. At the age of eleven his favorite composer was Duke Ellington, which is not a sentence I could have written about any other child I've taught. We learned "Take the 'A' Train" by ear that year, and "A Night in Tunisia" and "Caravan." Clinton turned twelve and I introduced him to Herbie Hancock and Maceo Parker; at thirteen he spent several months learning, note for painstaking note, a piano rendition of Don Wilkerson's tenor sax solo on Ray Charles's recording of "Hallelujah I Love Her So."

"Do you know that the sax player improvised that solo?" I asked Clinton.

"Yes," said Clinton, who is a man of very few words.

"I mean, he's making it up as he plays it."

"Yes."

"Would you like to try improvising a little, while I play the chords?"

"No."

"You could use some of the notes the sax player used, and just kind of mix them up a little."

Clinton decided to wax expansive. "No, thank you," he

said. He was looking at me as though I had suggested not only walking out on an airplane wing but jumping off. He simply had no idea how it was done. And I couldn't help him; I didn't know, either.

Fifteen-year-old Max and I arrived at the same impasse. Since tendering his formal resignation from classical music, he had worked his way enthusiastically through an intermediate lesson book called *Jazz Etudes* and a swanky arrangement of "Don't Get Around Much Anymore" when he heard a recording of Oscar Peterson and his trio playing "Summertime." It was by far the most momentous discovery of his musical life. He brought his iPod to a lesson and played it for me, sitting motionless and staring into space. "I have to play it," he told me.

"Max, it's really, really hard," I said.

"I can do it," he said.

Max began bringing his iPod to every lesson. I figured out—very, very slowly—how to play the introduction, eight bars of solo piano combining the silken sheen of jazz with the drawl and grit of the blues, and began to teach it to him. Quick-fingered and cocky, he was accustomed to learning music easily, and he was astonished at how difficult this was. "I thought I could do it," he said, chagrined.

"You will be able to do it," I told him, "but only if you play it very slowly, every day, over and over and over."

"Okay."

"*And over.*"

"Okay, okay."

Max went home and played the introduction over and over and over. It took him a month, but he learned it. We forged on, working through the first chorus of the tune; Max learned to play some vaguely jazz-voiced chords with his left hand and the melody in octaves with his right. We even figured out the sparkly little licks between the phrases. Then we came to Peterson's solo. We listened to it all the way through. I estimated that it would probably take me a year to figure out what Peterson was playing in those two astonishing choruses. Max sat, staring into space, waiting.

"Max," I said, "do you know that Oscar Peterson is improvising that solo?"

"Yeah," said Max, "so how do I do that?"

No teacher likes this moment. "I don't know how, Max," I said. "I can't really teach you about jazz improvising."

"Sure you can, just give it a try," he said, which is of course a sentence he learned, verbatim, from me.

I gave it a try, and so did he. But we didn't exactly crack the mystery of jazz improvising wide open. At some point I will have to turn Max over to a teacher who can help him play jazz. In the meantime, though, he did learn something crucial from me and Oscar Peterson. In a word—or five—he learned about "over and over and over."

Teaching kids how to practice is a central preoccupation

of every piano teacher during the intermediate stage. Unless we do this successfully, progress will become increasingly elusive, even for the most talented. And it is not a skill that comes naturally. Unless they are taught otherwise, students tend to think that practicing means playing each of their assigned songs once, as fast as possible and complete with exactly the same mistakes they made the day before, and then going off to play video games.

The problem, of course, is that there is absolutely nothing fun about practicing correctly. As anyone who has ever studied an instrument knows, there is no alternative to the profoundly tedious process of breaking a piece of music into small sections and playing those sections, much more slowly than you want to, over and over . . . *and over.* To a child who thinks he is taking piano lessons "for fun," this is a very tough proposition. It requires patience and a degree of self-discipline that is sometimes difficult to distinguish from masochism.

I remember my own gradual discovery of this reality, as a developing pianist. My teachers were quite clear on the fact that the Mozart concerto and the Rachmaninoff prelude could not be learned simply by playing from one end to the other; they had to be taken apart and acquired, through painstaking, sometimes infuriating repetition. "Over and over," said Mrs. Witschey, with her bright smile. "Over and over," said the forceful Madame Dmitrieff, the placid Mrs. Bane.

And now it is I who take my students through the process of correct practicing fairly frequently, in the hope that it will sink in. "Play it in slow motion," I will say, about a problematic phrase. "Slow motion," the first time, is usually not slow enough; there are still mistakes. "Slower," I say, "slow enough that it's perfect." Grimaces, always, but we eventually arrive at perfect. "Now do it five times at that speed," I say.

"Five times?"

"Five times perfectly. If you make a mistake, it doesn't count." Groans, often; histrionic wails every now and then.

"If you were really serious about it," I have been known to say, "you'd make it ten times perfectly *in a row*." Gasps and reproachful glares. The idea of quitting piano lessons is nearly visible in a balloon above the student's head.

Sooner or later, the offending passage is produced five times slowly and perfectly. Sooner or later, the student is usually able to see a concrete connection between the torturous process and the fact that the passage sounds much better than it did before. But it remains an open question whether that student will be able to repeat the process at home, alone at the piano, with no one to make her do it. "You have to be the student fingers and the teacher voice, both, when you're home," I say. "You, the teacher, have to say to you, the student, 'Five times perfect!' You have to make yourself do it. Do you think you can?"

I am aware that my question is more than pedagogical. I'm really asking something about the student's relation to herself. Is she able to forgo immediate gratification? Can she undertake a boring and uncomfortable task for the sake of achieving a goal? The capacity for self-discipline can't, by definition, be taught; it's an internal capacity that evolves slowly and privately. I can't impart it in a forty-five minute lesson. But I can provide a glimpse of how it would look, and what it would feel like. The rest happens, or doesn't happen, at home.

At home, of course, parents enter into the picture. And sometimes parents require a bit of training themselves. The dad who stands over his son calling out "C sharp!" and "Don't rush!" needs to be encouraged to find something to do in the kitchen during practice times. The mom who says "I couldn't care less if she practices, after all she's doing this for *relaxation*," on the other hand, might want to think about standing over her daughter now and then. For the most part, the parents of my students are wonderfully game and try hard to get the balance right. And of course it's impossible to get the balance right; we're talking about parenting, after all, the job we are all guaranteed to do wrong. As a parent of two children who took saxophone lessons for years and practiced less than I would have liked, I plead guilty to both "G flat, not G natural!" and "I couldn't care less," sometimes on the same day.

Trickiest to negotiate, with parents, is the question of talent. All parents want to believe that their children are talented. But not all parents' children are talented, of course, and this includes some of my students. Talent is unfair and undemocratic; it's also inarguable. I am consistently impressed with how easily talented children perform tasks that intelligent, dedicated, less talented children struggle with for years. So when a parent asks me, "Do you think he's got talent?" I am usually pretty certain about what I think, especially if it's an intermediate-level child with whom I have been working for a few years.

"Yes, he's got talent," I answer whenever I honestly can. But what am I to say when Karen is not especially talented? Karen is growing, I say, she is progressing, developing new capacities. Platitude heaped upon cliché, but also true. More often than not, I say, "Karen is finding her musical identity." That may sound pretentious as well as platitudinous, but it's the answer I can deliver most wholeheartedly. Because in fact it's my favorite aspect of the intermediate, emerging stage. For most students, the gradual discovery of musical taste and identity is perhaps the central drama of this phase of learning. It goes along with, and helps to foster, the developing sense of self. And every child can accomplish it, talented or not.

If the good folks at the Music Genome Project ever wonder about the formation of that individual musical profile they work so hard to quantify, they would do well to look at children from around the ages of ten to fifteen. These are the years when kids are discovering just what moves and interests them, musically speaking—what they like to listen to, what they like to play, what they are instinctively drawn to and what leaves them cold. It's a mysterious process, almost alchemical I sometimes think, and fascinating to witness.

The whole concept of individual musical taste is a fairly modern phenomenon, of course. In precommercial cultures, when music was imbedded in communal and religious life, there wasn't much question of individual taste or preference; everyone had the same exposure to the same music, more or less, as everyone else. The idea that musical taste could be an aspect of individual personality, definable on a Facebook page or a college application form, would have been incomprehensible.

Now, though, the ubiquity of recorded music means that we can each pick and choose not only among all the genres of modern music but also among all music that was ever written. Madonna, bluegrass, Gregorian chant, Tupac, ragas, Nat King Cole, Palestrina, the Beach Boys—is it really possible not to be overwhelmed by the sheer volume of choices?

It must be possible, because I see many of my students move through this crowded universe and find their way to the music that intrigues and delights and invigorates them.

The creation of a personal musical universe happens to be easier than ever before, thanks to the invention of the Internet and the iPod; kids, like adults, use their iPods to construct their own musical neighborhoods out of the vast territory of what's available. And—it bears repeating—what they come up with tends to be almost magically idiosyncratic. When I scroll through the tunes on their iPods, I always expect to be surprised by the juxtapositions and combinations, and I am usually not disappointed. Amy's library of music includes the Broadway show *Hairspray*, the pop group Maroon 5 and the country line-dance "Cotton-Eye Joe"; Max's beloved Oscar Peterson (if iPods had grooves, these would be well-worn) is followed by "Bohemian Rhapsody." How to explain precisely what moves each child? I prefer to think of musical preference as something finally irreducible, unpredictable and inarguable as a thumbprint.

I especially love the fact that many kids can't be pegged as "popular" or "classical"; given some exposure to classical music, they persist in enjoying both. My own sons, for example, display spectacularly catholic musical tastes. Evan listens to Ravel and Holst, Artie Shaw and Duke Ellington, the rap group Jurassic Five, the fusion banjo player Béla Fleck, the pop/soul singer India.Arie, the minimalist composer Steve Reich . . . have I mentioned his barbershop quartet phase? Adam loves bluegrass and classic rock, Stravinsky and Satie; he listens to Robert Randolph's funk and soul, Bill

Evans's jazz piano, the soul crooner John Legend. Because they are both so deeply and constantly engaged with music, their adventures of discovery among and across musical genres are particularly wide-ranging.

But I find many of my students adventurous in this regard as well. Tanya, for example, who struggled so heroically with the *Moonlight* Sonata, is a big fan of both Alicia Keyes and Coldplay, and has recently expressed an interest in Brahms. There is Pia, who loves Chopin waltzes and songs by Enya; there is Christopher, who loves U2 and Mozart. And the Debbie who was enchanted by a Shostakovich piano concerto is the same Debbie who introduced me to the Ben Folds Five band. I think the odds are pretty good that she is the only piano student in the United States who played Shostakovich and Ben Folds Five at her piano lessons last year.

Back to Karen, who actually is, as I have assured her parents, finding her musical identity. Over the past year Karen's technique did not improve; her sight-reading skills remained modest, to put it mildly; she did not effectively master a single piece of music. But she and I discovered together that she really likes the music of Louis Armstrong and Johann Strauss. And that's a discovery worth making. She would have made it without piano lessons, of course, but probably not by the age of twelve.

"What would you rather play in the recital, Karen," I ask

her in May, relishing the very sound of the question, " 'Stompin' at the Savoy' or *The Blue Danube Waltz?*"

Karen closes her eyes and frowns. "I think we'll be out of town that day," she says.

I would love her to play both, of course, but I know when not to ask. "*The Blue Danube*, then," I say, "you play it so well."

She opens her eyes. A look of confidence crosses her face, followed by doubt, followed by confidence ... "*Blue Danube*, sure," she says, "unless we happen to be out of town."

CHAPTER FIVE

Mastery

*W*hen I was fifteen my family moved from Westchester to New Jersey. It was the last of a series of moves necessitated by my father's rise up the corporate ladder of what used to be called, in the quaint phrase of a simpler time, the phone company. My mother, as she had so often done before, began an exhaustive reconnaissance of our new location in pursuit of the perfect pediatrician, orthodontist, hairdresser, car mechanic, tennis club, shoe store, skating rink and swimming pool. As she always did, she gave particular attention to the quest for the perfect flute teacher for my younger sister Leslie and the perfect piano teacher for me. My youngest sister, Paige, loved music—was very much attached, in fact, to the little record player she had inherited from me—but decided early on that she would rather listen to her sisters play than struggle with her uncooperative viola; for her, therefore, my mother was required to find the perfect riding stable. She found it, of course, a picture-perfect little establishment of white picket fences and emerald meadows called Tranquility Farms. For Leslie's lessons, it was a simple matter of landing a flautist from the New Jersey Symphony.

I was a more difficult proposition. I had grown choosier as I became more advanced; and I was, after all, a teenage girl. I took a trial lesson or two with a number of excellent teachers and pronounced Mr. Bernstein too excitable, Mademoiselle Coombs too rigid, Mr. DeGray too far away. "There's a young woman named Anita Gordon," said my somehow-undaunted mother. "I've heard she's good."

Mrs. Gordon had light blue eyes clear as lake water, a beautiful aquiline nose, an easy smile and astonishing fingers; merely watching her play a scale during the first lesson, I knew I was in the presence of real virtuosity. The scale was meant to demonstrate something about arm and wrist position, but it was those fingers—perfectly curved, effortlessly fleet, lithe and muscular at the same time—that made an impression. "I think she'll be okay," I told my mother.

Mrs. Gordon had a Steinway grand at the end of her living room, which was sparely furnished and always immaculate. She had two winsome little boys, an eminent professor husband, a steady flow of amiable students; she made being a grown-up look utterly enjoyable. Her four-year-old son played sweetly and silently with Legos in a nearby playroom while she gave lessons, so among the many things I learned from Mrs. Gordon was the revelation that motherhood was effortless.

More to the point, one of the first things I learned in the lessons was that music could be spoken of in architectural terms. Mrs. Gordon insisted upon my understanding the thematic structure of a Mozart sonata, the harmonic plan of a Brahms intermezzo. I was unsettled by this, finding it unnecessarily theoretical and more than a little confusing. Was it really necessary to unpack the structural secrets of a piece in order to play it well? Mrs. Gordon maintained that it was, talking me through the modulations of a Chopin nocturne while in the playroom little Josh pondered complex Lego creations. There was a taste for the abstract satisfactions of structure in this family, I thought, that I could not hope to match.

I soon found, however, that Mrs. Gordon was every bit as interested in the tangible, physical aspects of playing the piano as she was in the enchantments of musical construction. She paid a great deal of attention to my wrists and elbows, my neck and back; all of these had to be properly positioned and aligned and yet relaxed. I had always assumed that forceful playing required tense muscles, but Mrs.

Gordon made it clear that power at the piano required a vigilant relaxation; she was dedicated to abolishing tension whenever it appeared, which in my case seemed to be fairly often. I had never realized that my pinky was excessively curved or that I had a habit of tightening my forearm muscles when playing difficult passages, or indeed that these things mattered. Once, confronted by a series of spiky broken octaves in some Beethoven sonata, I grew frustrated that I could not play them fast enough. "Too much tension in your arms," she said. I made a conscious effort to relax my arm muscles. Sure enough, the octaves went faster. "You can't be in control of your playing," she said, "unless you relax."

Mrs. Gordon, I decided, must have achieved some Platonic ideal of relaxation, because she had a positively stunning degree of pianistic control. She did not play for me frequently—I was in the hot seat most of the time during our lessons—but I was energized and inspired when she did. She could produce a dozen gradations of "soft," a dozen versions of "loud"; she knew at least a dozen ways to get from one to the other. She could articulate the three melodic layers of a Bach invention as clearly as if three people were singing them. She could go from fast and tempestuous to slow and tender in an instant; she could even render slow and tempestuous, or fast and tender. And she expected no less from me.

My lessons with Mrs. Gordon gave me my first clear image of musical mastery. I knew what mastery sounded like, of course; my cherished childhood forty-fives had been replaced by an equally cherished collection of LPs, and I listened to Serkin playing Beethoven, Rubinstein playing Chopin, a formidable Hungarian woman named Edith Farnadi playing Rachmaninoff. I heard Ashkenazy and Barenboim and Pollini in concert; I once shook Andre Watts's hand. But those versions of mastery were in another realm altogether; they had nothing to do with me. In Mrs. Gordon's living room, on the other hand, when I got up from the piano bench and she sat down, I experienced firsthand and close-up exactly what constituted masterful playing: the technical fluency, the clarity of articulation, the range of emotional expression. And when she got up and I sat down again, I knew, in a very palpable way, what to try for.

What I did not know then—what I know now, from my own teaching—was the energy and inspiration an accomplished, ambitious student can give back to her teacher. Since I am a community piano teacher rather than a faculty member of a conservatory or music institute, I have had relatively few students capable of aiming for mastery at the piano. But I have consistently found that these few are invigorating, as well as touching, in a very particular way; I experience them as vividly as I experienced Mrs. Gordon all those years ago.

Advanced students, after all, are usually students who have made a discovery about themselves: they have realized that they love to play the piano. Some might even say they *have* to play the piano. They are not taking lessons, as are so many beginning and intermediate students, because it's fun, or because they have a knack for it, or because their parents want them to or because they like me (not to mention the jellybeans and the beagle). They are in this because of an attraction to the act of playing that is compelling, deep and inarguable.

This doesn't mean they will become concert artists; almost certainly they won't. It means simply that they feel an internal necessity to play, and to play well. They have experienced the sheer physical pleasure of technical facility and the soul-stirring elation of expressive power, and they have discovered that these satisfactions are somehow essential to their lives. As a teacher, I can't take credit for the discovery; it comes entirely from within. I can only witness it, and rejoice.

It happened fairly recently to Eddie, the teenager who loves Christmas carols and minor chords. Eddie's adventures in reading music began with his big book of Christmas carols but did not end there; an equally big book of Billy Joel tunes caught his attention next, and from all those rock-laced arpeggios it was not such a great leap to *Für Elise*, which he rendered with considerable style and great delight. "It's cool," he said, "what else did he write?"

I knew that Eddie was very fond of music, but I did not

anticipate, when I put Volume One of the Beethoven piano sonatas in his hands, where it would lead him. He went home and began to sight-read those sonatas, and before long—there is no other way to put it—they were necessary to him. The volume became dog-eared virtually overnight, and bristled with bright green Post-its marking the pages that especially struck his fancy. What struck his fancy most of all was the *Pathétique* Sonata, one of Beethoven's most passionate and majestic works. I agreed to help him learn it, although with some misgivings; Eddie is a large fellow who has trouble fitting his fingers between the black notes, and his technical capacity was not great. I knew that he loved to sight-read, but I wasn't sure how he felt about hard work.

It was a critical question, because to strive for mastery at the piano, or any instrument for that matter, is really to re-define one's definition of "hard." Difficult passages must be broken down into their smallest parts and played—well, you know: over and over and over. When you think you cannot bear to play a passage one more time, you play it ten more times. Or twenty. If you have not maintained a meticulous, painstaking precision throughout those twenty times, you repeat it twenty times more. When you are tempted to give up and go make yourself a sandwich, there is no coach to stop you; you must be trainer and athlete, good cop and bad, all at once. It's a tall order for a disciplined grown-up, much less for a fifteen-year-old boy.

Eddie was determined, but determination is often inadequate to this kind of challenge. Fortunately, he was also possessed. He practiced his sonata so much that his technique, and even the physical qualities of his hands, began to change. His thumbs became more flexible, more willing to be tucked under his third or fourth fingers during sixteenth-note runs. His fourth and fifth fingers became stronger, so that melody lines were smoother. Watching him play parallel octaves, I had the impression his fingers had actually lengthened. Before my very eyes, and in relatively short order, Eddie became an advanced student. He was ready to address the challenge many students never contemplate, the challenge at the very heart of the enterprise: enlisting technique in the service of expression and feeling.

The first movement of the *Pathétique* begins with a crash—a great C-minor chord played in the darkness of the lower registers—followed by a somber, broken fragment of chords and melody, whispered as though in the shadow of the first chord. Eddie was enraptured by this opening and played it with real mastery, his newly nimble fingers moving securely between the chords with their jagged dotted rhythms. As he played his way into the heart of the movement, though, he could not always find the expressive through-line, much less the nuances; he charged through it, grabbing a forte here, a ritard there, in a take-no-prisoners fashion. He was, after all, fifteen, and he had not grown up listening to classical music; he had neither emotional experience nor aural image to guide him.

This was especially apparent when he came to the second theme of the sonata, a brisk, lilting little tune beginning low on the keyboard (played by crossing the right hand over the left) and continuing in a higher register. The tune appears first in a minor key and then later, and sweeter, in major. Then an angular four-note phrase in the bass clef interrupts the melody twice, chasing it to a different key with each interruption. Eddie ploughed through this section dexterously but mechanically, determined to get to the other side.

"Eddie," I said, "listen to the conflict here. The melody keeps trying to sing, but it gets interrupted . . ."

"Uh-huh," said Eddie.

". . . so it starts again, and gets interrupted again, and finally it prevails, and then there's this wonderful E-flat-major cadence."

"Mm," said Eddie.

"These interruptions and key changes—they're exciting, but they're unsettling. So the music feels more and more agitated as it drives toward that E-flat chord. See what I mean?"

Eddie reached for a jellybean, and I realized that fifteen years are probably not enough to experience the kind of magnificent turmoil that is the abiding subject of Beethoven's music. "Get up for a minute," I said, and I sat down on the piano bench and played it for him.

Voice teachers often talk about the importance of singing for their students, giving them a sound to imitate. Eddie understood the words I was saying, but was unable to imagine how those ideas might actually be expressed; he needed a sound to imitate. And when I got up and he sat down, he knew—just as I had known all those years before, on Mrs. Gordon's piano bench—what to try for. He played the passage again, and this time there it was: sweetness, turbulence, resolution. I had the sense that Eddie was perhaps experiencing this particular emotional struggle for the first time— experiencing it through the music. Through playing, he was actually learning a new way to feel.

I remember having the same impression about Chloe, playing the C flat at the melancholy heart of *Clair de Lune*. Chloe was an animated, energetic teenager, brimming with confidence and talent. She was studying singing as well as piano and aspired to a career as a vocalist; she had a lovely voice and—at least as important in her chosen field—a definite gift for obstinacy. The force of her personality came through in her playing; she tackled Brahms waltzes and Gershwin show tunes with a muscular vitality. These strengths did not serve her quite so well when it came to that C flat, which is as subtle and delicate, as quintessentially French in its inflections, as Proust's madeleine. Wistful tenderness was not prominent in Chloe's emotional vocabulary; as with Eddie, I had to unseat her and play the passage myself before she had any idea what I was looking for. When she played it back to me, imitating even the physical gesture of my hand as I hovered over the note and then sank into it, I saw her catch her breath. The very act of making the gesture seemed to evoke within her a new capacity for tenderness, and for sorrow.

Like Eddie, Chloe was musically hungry. It was wonderful to introduce her to Debussy and Brahms, Mussorgsky and Dvořák, and to watch her as she learned to understand and express the humor and passion in the music. There was one area, though, where Chloe and I went head to head, and that was the issue of memorization.

Memorizing music is a challenge for instrumental students at every level. At the advanced levels it becomes both more challenging and more important—challenging, because the pieces are longer and more complex, and important, because without memorization there can be no mastery. Chloe was not alone in finding this process formidably difficult; it's my impression that for nearly every student, committing a long musical work to memory—requiring, as it does, a state of constant, fluid communication between body and mind—is one of the hardest things he or she has ever done. We memorize music with our finger muscles and also with our wrists, our arms, our feet on the pedals. At the same time, we memorize music with our heads—our visual memory, our auditory memory, our rational understanding of the internal workings of the music. All of these ways of remembering have to be engaged, just about all the time, or the piece is not truly memorized.

Chloe, to whom many things came easily, was miffed by the difficulty of memorizing music. She did manage to memorize *Clair de Lune* and to perform it in a June recital so beautifully, complete with a truly heartbreaking C flat, that not only her parents wept, but so did mine, who did not even know her. Justifiably pleased with her performance, she declared herself to be in a Debussy phase, and the following year, her senior year in high school, took on the Arabesque in E Major. It's a gorgeous piece that wanders through one shimmering tonal landscape after another, and Chloe found every trace of sun and shadow, of loveliness and yearning, there was to be found. Listening to her play it, I recalled that when she was eleven or twelve, she and my older son Adam had played a duet, an arrangement of *Humoresque* for piano and saxophone. She had been all bounce and chutzpah; what she lacked in subtlety she made up for in gusto. And now here she was, rendering the exquisite tints of Debussy's music; I would never have guessed she was capable of such expressive depth.

But she would not memorize it.

So when she announced to me that she had decided to

play the Arabesque in a town piano recital sponsored by a consortium of local teachers, I was surprised. We hold these recitals jointly, once a year; each teacher submits several students, who must audition for another teacher before they are eligible to participate. Chloe had scheduled an audition with Marni, a piano teacher across town. "Chloe," I told her, "one of the recital rules is that pieces have to be memorized. Marni may not approve you if you can't play it by memory."

Ah, to be seventeen. "It won't be a problem," she said, "I'll just tell her I'm going to."

She arrived at her next lesson sputtering. "I can't believe it," she said, "that teacher is so *stupid*. She says I have to come back next week and prove to her that I've got it memorized."

"Let's get started," I said.

She began to play. Her fingers knew the opening section flawlessly, automatically, but then she faltered. I explained to her that when muscle memory fails, one needs a fallback— either a visual image of the notes on the page or an understanding of what the music is made of, and preferably both. I told her about the great pianist Walter Gieseking, who used to write essays for himself about what happened, measure by measure, in music he was trying to memorize. I talked her through exactly what happened, harmonically and melodically, in the next section of the Arabesque, and I made her repeat it after me. "That's what you have to do now, Chloe," I said, "with the entire piece."

"Okay," said Chloe. One need not be a teacher—one need only be a parent—to know when "Okay" means "In your dreams."

Marni called me after Chloe's second audition. "I'm sorry," she said, "but I cannot support her playing in the recital. She has not memorized the piece."

There were tears at the next lesson. The teacher was stupid, the rule was stupid, the recital was stupid. "Chloe," I managed to interject, "there are still three months to go before my own recital in June. So you can play it then. You'll have plenty of time to memorize it."

"Okay," said Chloe.

That one was a bit more enigmatic—somewhere between "I guess so" and "Do I have to?" But I was resolved; she had to. I wanted her to shine in her last recital with me. So did her parents—not to mention mine.

Obstinacy, in the form of adolescent defiance, can drive piano teachers crazy no less than parents. It's hard to watch a talented student get in her own way for the sake of sheer noncompliance. But—and this is often easier for a teacher than for a parent to see—the very quality of stubbornness that sometimes undermines a student's progress can, at other times, be the bedrock of her strength as a developing musician. There are ways in which finding one's musical voice depends not on compliance but on holding fast to an insistent individuality.

I think of Pia, who came to me for lessons at the age of ten upon the recommendation of her babysitter—none other than Chloe, as a matter of fact. Pia's father told me before I met her that she was very gifted. He was indulging in understatement. Pia's technique was still developing but her ear was extraordinary; she could listen to complex melodies and harmonies and reproduce them exactly, her fingers moving across the piano keys as though over a Ouija board until she found, through an uncanny mixture of perception and intuition, the correct notes to play. I could see that for Pia, as for few others, the world was musically charged. She heard everything; she registered and remembered everything she heard. She would begin lessons by playing me the score of a movie she had just watched, or the musical hook of a video game she had just played or whatever bathetic pop song she had just heard in the supermarket. She worked out her own piano arrangements of all four of Vivaldi's *Seasons* and delighted in playing them, end to end, for anyone who would listen.

I relished the prospect of guiding Pia through what she would surely experience as the sumptuous delights of the piano literature. I discovered quickly, however, that Pia's musical likes and dislikes were as intense and intractable as her ear was keen. "I *hate* Mozart," she informed me, "and I *hate* Haydn. And I *really, really hate* Clementi." Well, this still left me a fair amount of room to maneuver; but I proceeded to learn that in fact there was a lot of Beethoven she didn't like, either, and quite a bit of Schumann, and vast acres of Bach. I experienced a profound sense of relief when Pia met her first Chopin waltz. Her technique was greatly challenged, and she complained that her hands hurt, but she loved it. She learned one waltz after another, scrambling after the notes and capturing them through sheer determination; her renditions of these wonderful pieces were not always polished, but they were, always, impassioned.

Pia has become somewhat more flexible as she has grown more technically proficient. There is, as it turns out, a Beethoven sonata that is not half bad. Debussy seems to have written a few cool pieces. Pia has even been game—briefly—for trying a bit of Scarlatti. But she remains consistently and ardently strong-minded.

This can be frustrating when her opinions involve matters about which I know a great deal more than she does. There are times when I engage, despite my better judgment, in power struggles over the meaning of a tempo marking or the appropriateness of a fingering choice. There are times when she simply has no interest in what I have to say. When she first played me her composition *Lullaby for the Moon*, I was effusive in my enthusiasm but ventured to make a suggestion. "You might want to think about preparing for that key change," I said, "for example with a dominant seventh chord. Sometimes an unprepared key change can sound like a mistake."

"I would *hate* a dominant seventh chord there," said Pia, "that is the worst idea *ever*." Sometimes I am very tired after a lesson with Pia.

And yet without her obstinacy, her insistent opinions, would she have composed it at all? Probably not. Creating something original requires a fierce willingness to be different. And Pia has been composing music since I met her. There was a song inscrutably titled "Soñadora"; there was a sonata in two movements, composed the week after I explained sonata form. There was a Broadway-style show tune, complete with hyperactive lyrics sung over her shoulder as she played. With every one of her compositions Pia takes a risk; there is always a moment when she doubts herself and fears that what she's done is no good. It's her stubborn streak that pulls her through those moments. Pia is bound and determined to create herself musically. It's not an easy job, and a bit of bullheadedness can only help.

Clinton, who is exactly Pia's age, is equally determined. But he could not be more different in style, personality and musical preference. He is as reserved as she is voluble, as painstaking as she is spontaneous; his tastes, as we have seen, extend from Bach to Ray Charles by way of Ellington, whereas Pia wants as little as possible to do with jazz, not to mention Bach. In recitals they often play one after the other, and I marvel at the difference in the very sounds they produce.

There is a great deal of talk in pianistic circles about "tone," and the mysterious and ineffable differences between the tones produced by different pianists. I have always taken a somewhat skeptical view of this discussion. A piano sound is produced by pressing a key, which activates a hammer, which strikes a set of strings; it seems to me that no matter how lovingly, aggressively or spiritually a key is pressed, the hammer will leap up and strike the strings just the same. Unlike a violinist, whose fingers press directly upon her vibrating strings, or a clarinet player, whose lips pulse against his vibrating reed, a pianist basically operates a row of levers. How then can one pianist sound so different from another?

Yet we do, undeniably, sound different—and there is no more dramatic proof than listening to Clinton play after Pia; logically impossible though it may be, the same piano that sang bright and sharp for Pia is dark, deep and lustrous in Clinton's hands. And the "tone" of both is remarkably consistent; Clinton produces a similar sound on my piano and on his, and he has done so ever since he conquered *Spanish Fiesta* at the age of nine.

Clinton, like Pia, has made tremendous technical strides in the last few years. And like Pia, he is evolving toward mastery along his own highly individual path. There are many pieces, both classical and jazz, that he simply will not play (most of them happen to be in major keys). But to the pieces he likes, he gives himself completely. He approaches Mozart's *Turkish Rondo* with no more meticulous attention than he devotes to "Hallelujah I Love Her So"; a pop ballad by a trendy R & B crooner receives the same elegance of execution as a Debussy prelude. For a while now I've wanted him to try his hand at a sonata, but it is difficult to guide Clinton in the matter of repertoire; his preferences are strong and precise. "The next two things I want to learn," he announced recently, "are 'Take Five' and the Habañera from *Carmen*." Well, and why not?

"That's fine, Clinton," I say, "and I also want you to start learning a Beethoven sonata."

He considers. "As long as it's in minor," he allows.

So I introduce him to the F-Minor Sonata, one of the first ones I played at his age. He likes the way the first movement begins, stern and playful at the same time, but he is daunted by all those pages ahead; he's never played anything so long. I explain to him that the length is manageable because it's put together according to the rules of sonata form, one of the most expressively powerful musical constructions ever invented. My enthusiasm on this point meets with a blank stare, and I remember that, at fifteen, I was similarly unable to join Mrs. Gordon in her passion for the particular delights of musical form. It wasn't until a few years later that

I understood what she was talking about—thanks to another music teacher, one utterly different from Mrs. Gordon but equally inspiring.

And in fact Bill Heyne should not go unmentioned in an account of my musical education, although he did not teach piano at all. Mr. Heyne was the choral director at my all-girls' high school, and I cannot imagine what the school authorities, charged with safeguarding the virtue of young womanhood, were thinking when they hired him. He was middle-aged—in his forties, I seem to think—with flamboyantly dyed blond hair, carefully honed pectorals and bright blue eyes; when he laughed, which was often, every girl in chorus felt that she had just heard something she was not supposed to hear. The fact that he was an extraordinary and passionate musician made us doubly motivated to sing for him as beautifully as we possibly could.

When I reached the spring of my senior year, it was clear to me that my spring independent project should be a tutorial with Mr. Heyne. Mr. Heyne decided that we should analyze sonata form, which was fine with me; as I recall, anything would have been fine with me. We sat under a tree outside the music wing, surrounded by thick yellow volumes of Mozart and Haydn and Beethoven, and while it is difficult to act out a sonata, that is, more or less, what he did. "The first and second themes are the main characters," he told me, "and they are introduced in separate keys, as though they live in different worlds." He would sing two themes in his grand voice, exaggerating the differences. "But in the development section they have these tremendous adventures together, journeying through different keys, different rhythmic escapades, until at last, at the end, they are able to come blissfully home to the same key!" Well, blissful it certainly was to bask in the May sunshine with Mr. Heyne and his twinkling eyes; but I found myself actually excited, in fact, by his vision of the dramatic potency inherent in the very structure of the music. When I heard the following year that he had, inevitably, run off with a student, my pang of jealousy was only brief. She had a romantic elopement, to be sure, but I had a revelation about the sensuous drama of sonata form; and as things turned out, mine was by far the more enduring experience.

Someday, surely, Clinton will have a similar revelation. Perhaps it will come not from his piano teacher but from some fascinating and glamorous new influence, as it did for me. In the meantime, though, he plays the beginning of the F-Minor Sonata better and better every week. He may not quite get the structural drama of themes and keys, but he gets that it's beautiful, and that its beauty depends on precision.

The elegance of Clinton's playing is a reflection of his personality; there is a seriousness and poise about this boy unusual for a young teenager. It's also connected, I think, with his gifts as an athlete. Athletic talent isn't necessary for musical skill, of course. But in Clinton, as in many other musical children—including my sons—I can see that it helps; performing a Mozart sonata requires hand-eye coordination, physical grace and rhythmic intuition no less than dribbling a basketball down the court and taking a shot. Clinton plays basketball—and lacrosse, and baseball and soccer—avidly and well. I know this from talking to him and to his parents, but I might have guessed it from the way he tosses off a hand-over-hand arpeggio.

It's interesting that my other jazz-loving teenage student, Max, is also an athlete. I've never seen him play tennis, but from watching him play "Summertime" à la Oscar Peterson, I would bet he's strong, adept and bold. Although he struggled at first with Peterson's rippling, blues-edged runs and monstrous jazz chords, he plays them now, finally, with considerable agility and at top speed. I'll bet Max likes to play singles.

If he practiced consistently the way he practiced "Summertime," Max would be on the way to mastery at the piano. But he is not possessed, like Eddie, or in thrall to a music-saturated world, the way Pia is; the piano for Max is stimulating but not quite necessary. After we hit the wall with "Summertime," I resolve to assign him something challenging yet accessible (and nonclassical; his rule on that issue remains ironclad) and come up with Billy Joel's *Root Beer Rag*, a piano composition that combines ragtime charm with a rock swagger and lots of sixteenth notes. He eyes it suspiciously. "My little brother likes Billy Joel," he advises me.

"This is not 'Piano Man,' Max," I tell him, "it's a real piano piece, and by the way, it goes really fast."

"Show me," he says, getting up, and I sit down and play the beginning of it as fast as I can. "If you think it might be too hard, maybe your brother will want to try it," I offer as my parting shot.

"I'll do it, I'll do it," says Max.

He learns the first page of *Root Beer Rag* and plays it again and again, faster every time, taking an athletic delight in the sheer physical experience of playing fast, playing loud, playing hard. But the next five pages pose greater technical challenges, and a passage of swift parallel octave chords in the right hand has him stymied. "Max," I tell him, "this part is even more fun, once you learn it."

Max decides to blame Billy Joel. "I don't get why he made it so hard, with those octaves," he says. "It would sound just as good if I just played the top notes."

I was never a competitive athlete, but I clearly remember my discovery, as a teenager, that the more skill I acquired at the piano, the more playing felt like sport—physically exhilarating, energizing, risky. I remember playing Debussy's *Doctor Gradus ad Parnassum* and feeling like wind was whistling in my ears. And I remember asking Mrs. Gordon why the piece so frequently involved flying the left hand back and forth across the right, from the lowest octaves to the highest notes; it seemed to me the piece could be played perfectly well with the left hand taking care of the low notes and the right hand the high ones.

No, said Mrs. Gordon, the flying hand is essential. It looks great to the audience. And it feels great to play.

"No," I say to Max now, "the octaves are essential. They feel great to play."

He looks interested, if not quite convinced. "Really?"

"Like smashing an overhead," I say. Max rolls his eyes; it's as corny as something his parents would say. But it works. He starts practicing those octave chords.

Haley probably thinks it's corny, too, when I invoke athletic analogies. Haley came to me, you may recall, to play fun stuff, and stayed to play Chopin and Debussy and Schubert—and to play them marvelously, with increasing skill and finesse; she's very talented, and because she's also diligent, her technique is as strong as her talent is deep. Haley plays on the high school softball team; she is tall and strong, with a high flush in her cheeks, and I can imagine her slamming one out of the park, which is why I am surprised the first time I hear her play the stormy middle section of her Schubert Impromptu. She plays it carefully, diffidently; all the notes are correct, but this music is dark and fierce and requires a degree of brute force. "You need to use the same muscle strength as when you play softball," I tell her. "Right now you're only playing it with your hands. You need to play it with your arms, your back, your chest, everything."

She's too polite to roll her eyes, but she looks uncomfortable, almost angry. At home, though, in private, she's able to try taking the risk. Each week her rendition of the section is stronger, and eventually she is able to hurl herself at the chords so they peal like thunder. Haley is a good girl, conscientious and eager to please; it's possible she's never made such a din. But now that she has, thanks to the confluence of Schubert and softball, I am eager to see her continue. I think of Mrs. Witschey, in her white linen, playing with force and vitality; of Madame Dmitrieff urging me, at thirteen, to play deep, deep! I think of Mrs. Gordon suggesting to me, at fifteen, that I might aspire to power as well as grace, and I visualize her at the piano, playing with an explosive vigor that transformed my image of what a good girl could do. And I would love to pass on to Haley the permission I received from those splendid women to make powerful, vigorous music. I consider what to assign her next: Beethoven? Tchaikovsky? Rachmaninoff? "The *Maple Leaf Rag*," I find myself saying, "I want you to learn the *Maple Leaf Rag*."

It's not what she had in mind, either; but she agrees—politely, as always. At her next lesson she hands me the music. "I memorized the first three sections," she says, and when she tears into the rag at breakneck speed, I realize why I had wanted her to play it. She doesn't think of it exactly as classical music, so she's able to be less polite, noisier. It's not at the expense of control, though; her accuracy is dazzling. My lecture about the correct way to practice a stride bass, to minimize mistakes, dies on my lips. Haley's not making *any* mistakes. I find myself wishing I could play it like that—a relatively unfamiliar sensation in my teaching experience, and one to relish. She finishes the third section with re-sounding octaves in both hands and looks at me, breathless; she has played so hard that her ponytail has come loose. "Scott Joplin played it faster," she offers.

"How do you know?"

"I found it on iTunes," she tells me, "he played it, like, impossibly fast."

I explain to her that what she heard on iTunes might have been a piano roll, a mechanical reproduction played on a player piano, and that Joplin himself is known to have rec-ommended that pianists play his rags at a relaxed tempo.

"Not me," she says, "I like it *fast*." I can see she's heady with that wind-whistling-in-the-ears thing. And there may be more to it; Haley may be remembering that this is the very piece my most advanced student, Justin, who is three years younger than she, played—at breakneck speed—in the last June recital. Haley may be a good girl, but she has a solid competitive streak, and I wouldn't be surprised if she were at this moment entertaining an agreeable fantasy of playing the *Maple Leaf Rag* faster than Justin ever played it . . . much, *much* faster.

Nearly all of my students compare themselves with Justin. Despite his age, he's been an advanced player for a number of years, a perennial cause for alternating inspiration and despair among my other students. "Was he just born that way?" I sometimes hear after a recital.

No one, of course, is born with automatic mastery at the piano. But a number of Justin's stars are in fortunate alignment. His family is Japanese-American and has instilled in him both a deep respect for classical music and an impressive capacity for disciplined work. He has immense talent and is very smart, in a modest, matter-of-fact way. And he is an athlete; he fences competitively in tournaments at the national level.

He came to me for his first lesson at the age of six, seven years ago, with his Suzuki book in hand. He could read only a little of the music in that book; for a year or two I played every new piece into a tape recorder. Home he would go, with Suzuki book and cassette tape, and he would come back the next week knowing the piece. Once, when he forgot his tape, I played him his new piece during the lesson and told him I thought he would be able to learn it by reading the music. Sure enough, he came back the next week playing it perfectly. "Justin, that's great," I said, "you learned it from reading the notes!"

"No," he said, "I remembered what you played."

Justin did not say much during lessons—he still doesn't—and his responses to music were rarely verbal. He would never say that he liked this piece, or was excited by that one; if I asked him, the most I would get was a quick nod and a deft poke at the jellybean jar (Justin has an acute sweet tooth). Once he learned the pieces, though, there was no mistaking how he felt; he played them hungrily, avidly, with an absorption deeper than joy. By the time he was ten he was playing entire Mozart and Haydn sonatas as though they belonged to him.

A friend who directed the local county youth orchestra suggested that Justin perform as a soloist with the orchestra. "Do you know what a concerto is?" I asked Justin at his next lesson. He shook his head. "It's a long piece that you play with an orchestra, and you're the main player but the orchestra plays too. Would you like to try it?" He nodded his head and dove for the jellybeans.

He began to learn the first movement of Haydn's Concerto in D Major, and so did my friend's youth orchestra. There were challenges: an octave was still a stretch for Justin's small hands, and he had to slide halfway off the piano bench in order to reach the pedal. It never occurred to him to become frustrated by these difficulties. Memorizing the twenty or so pages of music did not seem to faze him, either; within less than three months he knew the whole movement by memory, although he had no idea how he knew it. His greatest challenge was the cadenza—the solo star turn near the end, when the orchestra drops out entirely and the pianist plays more freely, unencumbered by the necessity to keep to a strict beat. Justin, who met every technical challenge with equanimity, was confounded by this outbreak of freedom; he simply could not help but keep the beat. "You can slow down on this measure," I told him, "and you can pause at the end of that one, if you want to."

"Oh," said Justin.

"In Haydn's day," I pointed out, "pianists made up their own cadenzas. It's the place where you get to let go a little bit."

He frowned. Clearly, he did not want to slow down, could not consider a pause, and had absolutely no interest in letting go. He was, after all, ten; he wanted to ride the music, not drive it. "Is it okay if I just, you know, play?" he said.

I told him it was fine. And when he played with the orchestra for the first time, it was clear that he was having the ride of his life. He played easily, fluently, feeling the orchestra ebb and flow, swell and subside, behind and around the piano parts he knew and loved so well; at the end, typically wordless, he ran up and down the empty aisle of the concert hall five or ten times. When he performed it in concert, he was something of a sensation; no matter that the octaves weren't quite there or that the cadenza was in march time, the audience was captivated—by his precocity, by his composure and by the fact that as he played, the rude gulf between eighteenth-century Vienna and the twenty-first-century world of a small suburban boy simply disappeared.

Justin has matured greatly since then, emotionally as well as technically. He has grown into Beethoven and Chopin; he has braved Bach and embraced Joplin; and although he declines anything remotely jazz-inflected, he plays the heck out of "Allentown." Word of his pianistic skill has spread at the local middle school, where he is an eighth-grader, and he comes to me one day with a fistful of sheet music; the choral director has asked him to accompany her chorus concert. "When is the concert?" I ask him.

"Next week," he says, "the rehearsal's tomorrow." It's the first time I've ever seen him look worried.

When he shows me the music, I understand his apprehension; Justin has met his biggest challenge. These are pop tunes and show tunes with fairly complicated piano parts; to learn them on short notice requires a willingness to wing it—to fake it, one might go so far as to say. Justin cannot even imagine winging, much less faking, a piano performance. He struggles to play every single dotted rhythm in the bass line, every note in every knotty chord. "Justin," I say, "you can't go for perfection here. You have to keep the tempo and hit the downbeats. All the other notes don't matter so much; grab them when you can, let them go when you can't."

He doesn't answer, but I can see he's horrified. Let the notes go? Justin has spent years honoring every note on a musical page. It is almost physically painful for him not to play all the notes he sees. I persuade him finally to leave out an annoying left-hand figure in one especially insipid pop song, and simply to play the roots of the chords, in order to stay in tempo. He does it, but the effort clearly exhausts him. "Would you like to play Beethoven now?" I say.

A fervent nod. He is learning the *Moonlight* Sonata for my June recital—not the first movement, which is too lugubrious for his taste, but the third, a feverish romp through thickets of arpeggiated black notes and minor keys. He launches into it, struggling happily to grab every single note. I listen to him move from the dark frenzy of the opening section to the lyrical sadness of the second theme with an expressive sensitivity far beyond his years, and I wonder, not for the first time, how he knows what he knows.

And I wonder, as I often do about my advanced students, what he will do with his musical mastery when he grows up. There are precious few job openings for concert pianists. Here in the metropolitan area of New York there are probably thousands of aspiring virtuosi accompanying dance classes, teaching as adjuncts and playing in Holiday Inns. The prospects of a successful performing career and a decent income are slim at best for Justin, for Haley, for all piano students whose developing musical skills are so exciting and so touching to their teachers.

So what's in it for them, finally? Why work so hard at something that will probably never constitute a career? And why do their struggles and triumphs seem so absolutely important to me?

The answer, of course, has to do with beauty, and with feeling, and with the intimate and mysterious connection between the two. The great aesthetic philosopher Suzanne Langer had a theory that musical forms are similar to, and symbolic of, the forms of human emotion; while music does not, for example, directly express sadness, it evokes an internal experience that is resonant with sadness. "An artist expresses feeling," she wrote, "but not in the way a politician blows off steam or a baby laughs and cries . . . What he expresses is not his own actual feelings, but what he knows about human feeling."

When my students strive toward mastery, they expand and deepen what they know about human feeling. The vast challenges of technical development are always, finally, in the service of emotional exploration: discussing a three-against-two figure, one may suddenly find oneself discussing sorrow, and a fingering change can open the way to jubilation. Teacher and student take turns leading and following one another through the possibilities of feeling; it is a kind of intimacy all the richer for being mediated by the beauty of music.

Justin gallops his way to the end of the *Moonlight*'s third movement; like Clinton, he may not exactly parse sonata form, but he is obviously in on the spirit of thematic high adventure. There is a repeat indicated before the final bar, and he thumbs wildly back through the pages looking for the beginning of the section. "When you play this in the recital," I tell him, "you don't have to take that repeat."

He throws me a reproachful glance. It's one thing to tell him to leave some notes out of a pop tune; it's quite another, clearly, to suggest not playing every note Beethoven wrote, exactly the way Beethoven intended. "It's okay," he says, "I'll play the repeat."

I don't want to tell him that if he plays all the repeats his piece will be too long in relation to my other students' pieces, but I am in fact concerned on this point. "You might find it feels awfully long that way," I say.

"Oh, then I'll just play it faster," he says. As he leaves, jingling jellybeans in his pockets, I have no doubt that he will.

CHAPTER SIX

Recital

$\mathscr{I}$f you remember your piano lessons, chances are you remember your piano recitals. Perhaps you remember an occasion of particularly gratifying triumph or spectacular failure, or perhaps your memories blur into a sort of *Ur*-recital, the year-to-year variations disappearing from memory. Your fingers may be able to find their way to the first few notes of a recital piece you haven't played for thirty or forty years. Or it may be the shoes you wore that you re-member, the clicking sound they made as you took that long walk to the piano, or the glassy feel of the unfamiliar piano's keys or the beads of cold sweat that inevitably broke out on your palms.

It is an odd and archaic ritual, the student piano recital;

one can only speculate as to how and when it began. The tradition of piano lessons is as old as the piano itself, no doubt, but the ritual of the student recital seems to be a twentieth-century phenomenon. Renoir's girl in orange, Muenier's girl in pigtails, the pale staring boy in Matisse's dark reverie—these children are not, I think, preparing for a June recital appearance.

Recital performances of solo piano music by anyone, adult or child, were in fact rare until the nineteenth century. A single person playing a single instrument was considered too private and intimate an event for the concert hall; people went out to hear symphonies or operas, but stayed home to enjoy piano music. It was not until piano virtuosi like Franz Liszt came along, with their flowing locks and death-defying keyboard acrobatics, that a piano player alone on a stage was considered sufficient reason for an evening outing. And it was not until childhood, and child-rearing, acquired modern self-consciousness, and parents arrived at a curious collective agreement to gather in groups and listen to the fledgling performance efforts of one another's children, that the student recital appeared.

Since it appeared, though, it has proven to be an astonishingly hardy phenomenon. Teachers need it, to motivate students and show off their accomplishments. Parents want it, to assure themselves and each other that their children have in fact learned something demonstrable in public. Students—well, they accept it as necessary. The idea of a recital tends to be exciting in January, worrisome in April and terrifying in June.

Terrifying, because recitals are fraught with peril. The hands can tremble, the fingers can fumble on the keys, the foot can slip from the pedal; the notes, so painstakingly learned, can rise from the mind like a flock of birds from a field and simply, instantly, fly away.

At worst, a recital can feel like a catastrophe. I think, memorably, of Megan, who studied piano with me as a teenager some years ago, when my practice was still small enough that I held recitals in my home. Megan knew her Bach invention perfectly, but in recital stumbled halfway through. She started again, stumbled again, froze completely and fled from the piano in tears; she went running through the assembled guests in my living room, through my dining room and into my kitchen, where we could hear her, quite clearly, weeping. Her mother, a close friend of mine, was sitting in the audience; she threw me a look I will not forget and rose to take her home. Being an uncommonly brave and spirited girl, Megan agreed to play in the next recital, and played very well. She went on to attend a top college, captain her varsity lacrosse team, graduate with high honors and spend two years in Africa with the Peace Corps, but I would not be surprised if she still counts her recital breakdown as one of the most uncomfortable moments of her life.

And I think of Tara, who at the age of ten or eleven played a charming little piece by Telemann, effortlessly and without a single mistake, all through April and May. At the recital, she looked composed as she sat down at the piano. She continued to look composed as she stared quietly at the keys, but she did not lift her hands to play. As I watched her from the front row, my own hands began to sweat. I realized she had blanked; the music was gone, as though a hard drive had crashed. I approached her and whispered, C in the right hand, E in the left. She played those notes and stopped. Now C in the left hand, E in the right, I said. She played; she stopped. D and then G in the right, I said, realizing with a sinking heart that I did not remember what came next. She played the D and G and then, to my startled and intense relief, played the next note, and the next and the next. She played to the end perfectly and stood up to face the applause with a dumbstruck look on her face. And while this experience may not account for Tara's developing an emphatic preference for Joni Mitchell over Telemann, it's clearly the reason that, although she took piano lessons for seven more enjoyable years, she never again played in a recital.

Usually, recital mishaps are less disastrous. Mistakes are made and recovered from. Memory lapses are stared down. Each student comes, sooner or later, to the end of the piece and receives a genial round of applause. But the experience is never comfortable, often disquieting, and occasionally excruciating.

Why, then, do I hold recitals? Why continue to put my students through what is admittedly an ordeal, so that they, like you, will years from now sustain anxious memories of sweaty palms and slippery keys?

Well, for one thing, parents tend to expect it—and parents are, after all, my clients. It is a rare parent who does not enjoy seeing his or her child perform successfully. Parents may not, of course, find it equally enjoyable to sit through the rest of the recital; the standard parental response to other students' performances might be captured in the words of the great pianist Artur Rubinstein, who said, in another context, "When they play badly, I feel terrible. When they play well, I feel worse." But for most parents, competitive discomfort is usually outweighed by the excitement of their own children's accomplishments.

So I do it for the parents. More important, though, I do it for my students. There is simply no denying that most students practice harder when they have a public performance to prepare for. Even the most conscientious young pianist will usually settle for less than perfection if there is no performance goal in sight. But with a recital looming, even the most lackadaisical youngster will spontaneously decide to practice that troublesome passage until it's right. It's a rite of spring I particularly cherish: sometime around the middle of

May, my students start playing better. Recital pieces become less flawed, more polished, with every passing week, as each child pushes through competence toward his or her own capacity for mastery—a profoundly satisfying experience, and one rare enough in any of our lives.

I often wonder if I should encourage my students to participate in the elaborate "audition" system provided nationwide by the National Guild of Piano Teachers, wherein students perform regularly for panels of judges; there are sets of prescribed pieces for each skill level, and children are evaluated according to a precise and intricate rubric. The handbook published by the Guild of Piano Teachers heartily advocates this system as a way to "prevent aimless drifting at the piano." I have so far steered clear of the Guild auditions, as I am not a particular fan of grading rubrics when it comes to musical performance. (I may even be guilty of harboring a seditious belief in the creative possibilities of "aimless drifting at the piano.") But they would certainly provide more opportunities for the push to perfection. In their stead I've developed my own informal alternatives: I hold "playing parties" at various holidays, when various subgroups of students come to my house and play for one another. Playing parties are all-girl (by popular demand) on Valentine's Day, all-boy (by way of compensation) on St. Patrick's Day, and attended on Halloween by a magnificent assemblage of witches, devils, supermen and fairy princesses, not to mention the occasional left shoe or ham sandwich. While these sessions provide a measure of performance experience—just try to play *Pumpkin Boogie* without your tiara sliding off—it's only the June recital, which happens in a community hall with parents in attendance and without jellybeans or beagle, that really ratchets up the pressure toward excellence. And while kids are sometimes nervous at the holiday playing parties, it's only the June recital that evokes true, bona fide stage fright.

Stage fright is not a trivial business. There are few feelings more unnerving than the stomach-clenching sensation of sitting in the audience or in the wings waiting to play, wanting it to be over, wanting to flee, to be anywhere else. At the last minute the risk can feel intolerable, and it sometimes requires an arduous combination of courage, recklessness and surrender to throw oneself over the edge and begin to play.

I don't relish the fact that my students suffer stage fright. But I do want to see them discover the capacity to throw themselves over that edge. I want them to experience the possibility of moving through fear and encountering courage, to be startled and impressed by their own resources. Mostly, they do. When they falter, I try to encourage them to feel pride in the attempt. Sometimes, they do.

There is one more reason to hold recitals. One of my most vivid performance memories from childhood is related not to the piano but to the all-girls' summer camp I attended at the age of thirteen, where I was chosen during the very first week to be one of the poem readers at the weekly assembly. "Look through this anthology and find a poem that strikes you," said a strapping counselor with a ponytail, "and memorize it." What struck me, as it happened, was "O Captain! my Captain! our fearful trip is done . . ." The portentous tragedy of the subject, the lofty swell of the language, filled my thirteen-year-old soul with terrible joy; my very favorite line was "But O heart! heart! heart!" and I wondered how Whitman had ever thought of it. Came the big day, and the first girl up recited "Stopping by Woods on a Snowy Evening." Lightweight, I thought smugly. Then came a poem about nightingales, and then something about a host of daffodils . . . and it began to dawn on me that every single girl was reciting a poem about nature. Clearly, I had missed some crucial instruction about a nature theme. No sooner had this dreadful insight sunk in than it was my turn. I began, light-headed with mortification: "O Captain! my Captain! . . ."

"We can't hear you," called the ponytail. I kept going but could summon no more than an embarrassed whisper. Then I came to the magnificent line. I had practiced it so many times in a tone of full-throated anguish that by now the pathos was automatic, and I found myself bellowing "O heart! heart! heart!" in spite of my embarrassment—at which moment I realized that this poem was mine now. Its sublime and flamboyant despair and its drum-roll cadences were mine to give to this audience, none of whom knew it as I did. I felt my face relax and my voice grow stronger as I declaimed the final line of each stanza with strenuous gloom: "Lying *cold and dead*." Nature theme be damned; the captain lay dead upon the deck, and it was my story to tell.

It is this sense of ownership I'm after, for my students. I want each student to feel that there are a few minutes of musical whimsy or energy or loveliness that belong to her, that she has made her own and that she more than anyone else has the power to share with others. Having a musical gift to offer, even in the uncomfortable context of a recital, brings a sense of pleasure and potency that is deeper than fear or anxiety, competitiveness or even perfectionism. It accounts, I think, for why some students—many, in fact—surprise themselves by enjoying recitals. At best, a recital can feel like a celebration.

During the weeks before the recital, I try to prepare my students for every aspect of the event. We practice walking to the piano and sitting down. We practice positioning the hands before starting to play, and holding them in place while the last chord resonates. I discuss the idea of respect for the audience and their response, and we practice acknowledging applause after performing (although this is largely a useless exercise, forgotten in the heat of the moment, when kids are apt simply to bolt from the piano bench, duck their heads as if heading into a gale wind and sprint for their seats). We practice recital pieces on each of my two pianos; we practice in front of their parents and my sons and anyone else who happens to be around—including, more than once, the mailman. Sometimes I think all this preparation is helpful; at other times I think it only makes students that much more nervous. But I can't skip it; I want them to be as ready as they can be.

Save the Date! Piano Recital, June 17, 7 P.M.!
Family and friends welcome.
Refreshments to follow!

THE FLYERS GO OUT with my May bills and are, I hope, affixed with magnets to my students' refrigerators. I rent the hall and get the piano tuned and type up the programs. On the day of the recital I arrive hours ahead of time to position the piano, set up the folding chairs, prepare the post-recital refreshments. My parents—as if they have not gone to enough piano recitals in their lives—always show up with flowers. We adjust air conditioning, we put programs on seats. People begin to arrive. Parents carry video cameras and younger siblings; students are unusually clean. Some have even dressed up. I ask them to sit in the first few rows, and they comply—until I look away, when a few of the smaller ones slide out of their seats and scamper to sit with their parents.

I watch the hall fill up and notice with some interest that I am feeling utterly overcome with anxiety. I have performed in many kinds of venues, for many years. I have accompanied well-known singers in highly publicized concerts. I have played keyboards and sung to packed rooms in bars and cafés; I've directed musicals and led small instrumental groups. On every single occasion I felt stage fright, in varying degrees. But I don't think I was ever quite as nervous as I am now, at my students' recital. I'm responsible for putting all of these children in a position of great exposure, and I experience a fairly acute moment of wishing I hadn't. What if they fail and are musically traumatized for life? What if they undergo a collective meltdown, and the recital simply grinds to a halt? What if all the parents want all their money back?

Alas, there's no way out of it now. All my students are here—all except Karen, who has, it seems, managed to be out of town. I'm not surprised; I was never confident that we would actually hear *The Blue Danube Waltz* this evening. In what I think is a steady voice, I welcome the parents and students to the annual June recital, and announce that we will begin with Jenny.

Jenny is whiter than her patent-leather shoes. She has agreed with great reluctance to play in the recital, on the condition that she play *Big Ben*, which has nineteen notes.

Clearly, she's regretting it now—no more fervently than I'm regretting that I insisted. She approaches the piano as if sleepwalking. She is attired—well, it's not pink and green embroidery, but it's close: a smock dress of daffodil yellow, with yellow hair ribbons and a purse to match her shoes. She brings the purse to the piano and places it carefully on the bench next to her as she sits down. She smoothes her skirt. And then she plays a resounding and deliberate E . . . followed at length by a C . . . followed, after a while, by D and then G. It sounds, in fact, just like Big Ben striking the hour . . . very, very slowly. She forges on, one momentous note at a time. And then it's finished, and it's perfect. The applause lasts nearly as long as her piece. She stands, picks up her purse and walks back to her seat.

I am dizzy with relief. If Jenny has managed that, I think, any of us can manage anything. I decide that this will be a wonderful recital after all. My euphoria lasts exactly as long as Jenny's round of applause; little Maggie, who is up next (I order the program more or less according to age) is nowhere to be seen. Ah, but there is Maggie's mother gesticulating at me from the back of the hall, and there is Maggie in her lap. Maggie has worked very hard on her recital piece, but it's clear she has been ambushed by an attack of stage fright as brutal as it is sudden. I hope the other students haven't noticed. This kind of thing can be contagious.

Fortunately her brother Willy, who's up next, hasn't

caught the bug. He literally charges to the piano as his father crouches in the aisle with a video camera. Is it really possible to be this pleased about a recital? He beams at the audience and launches into a spirited rendition of Queen's "We Are the Champions," which he's been working on for months. "*And we'll keep on fighting—till the end . . . duh-duh-DUH*," I can hear him singing softly as he plays. I allow students to play a second piece if it's an original composition, and Willy, who is a relaxed and fluent young composer, has created for this occasion a piece entitled *They're Coming!* with enough crashing C-minor chords to make Beethoven jealous. As I watch him acknowledge his applause for "Champions" and tumble headlong into *They're Coming!* I wonder whether I myself ever felt quite so unabashedly joyful about performing in public. The famous pianist Charles Rosen wrote in his memoirs that the professional pianist's goal in performance is to create a musical object. Although Willy likes the applause, I think his joy comes precisely from the act of creating a specific, beloved musical object, no less tangible for being in time rather than in space. It's nice that his performance has been captured on videotape, for posterity and his bachelor party; but there's a kind of permanence to what he's done, even without the tape.

My ruminations upon the idea of the musical object continue when Ella gets up to play. She, too, creates something very specific: a medley she's put together interpolating the theme from the *New World* Symphony into a piece from her lesson book entitled *Canoeing in the Moonlight.* To my ears it sounds a bit odd, and Dvořák would have been surprised, to say the least; but it's her musical object, not mine—or, for that matter, Dvořák's. She plays it with remarkable composure, and she has blond curls and fleet fingers. Her audience is sold.

Mara is up next. She has been very nervous about this recital, and so I have asked Chloe, who babysits for her (Chloe seems to be babysitter at large to a number of musical children), to accompany her on "My Favorite Things." Clearly, it has helped; with Chloe next to her, she walks to the piano with something less than total panic on her face. She is dressed in a chic little recital outfit that includes a beret. "*One*-two-three, *one*-two-three," proclaims Chloe, and they are off. Mara begins tentatively but becomes bolder with Chloe's "*oom*-pah-pah" to buoy her tune; when she fumbles a couple of notes, Chloe, already a nimble musician, adjusts her bass part accordingly. They take a very classy bow, the two of them, and I make a mental note to consider a beret for my own next public performance.

Susie also has an accompanist; her father plays the guitar, and they have prepared a rendition of "American Pie." Susie's family—I have taught her two brothers as well—has developed what amounts to a tradition of playing together at recitals, in varying configurations. I am always amazed at how well they pull this off; siblings playing together can be a dicey proposition. Even the slightest inclination toward rivalry or resentment tends to become inflamed when brother and sister try to arrive at a double bar at the same time. My own youthful experience playing duets with my sister, Leslie, who played a lovely flute, was that when we were both playing well it was blissful, but when either of us made a mistake it was, very rapidly, hell.

Susie and her brothers are not immune to this phenomenon. I particularly remember a holiday recital when all three of them at one piano played an arrangement of Springsteen's "Santa Claus Is Comin' to Town." Rehearsals were, it must be said, red in tooth and claw: accusations, counteraccusations, shoves and a few furtive punches. But the recital performance was pure sweetness and light, with tiny Susie playing jingle-bell chords at the high end of the piano, then running around her brothers to play a low bass line during the bridge and finally running back again for the jingly ending. It brought down the house.

Her brothers have defected to baseball and soccer now, and so her father keeps the tradition alive by strumming along as she begins the tune: "*A long, long time ago* . . ." I have been worried that she will not be able to memorize the whole song (remember how long it is?), but she doesn't miss a note. Dad, on the other hand, is not quite sure where each chord goes. He looks vaguely confused, and I feel guilty; I should have rehearsed him more. But they come together quite nicely on the chorus. "*So bye-bye, Miss American pie . . .*" I am sure I hear a few audience members singing softly. With a song like this, it's close to impossible for us children of the sixties and seventies to resist turning even a piano recital into a sing-along.

Rebecca comes hesitantly forward; it's always hard to follow a father-daughter act, especially when they play a generational anthem. Rebecca, you will recall, loves to sing when she plays, and I have encouraged her to sing as she plays her recital piece, "Seasons of Love" from the musical *Rent*. She has firmly refused. "You don't sing at piano recitals," she told me.

"Sometimes at my recitals you do," I said, and told her about the time the irrepressible Chloe played and sang a medley of Gershwin tunes.

She looked horrified. "I would *never* do that," she informed me.

I am hoping that "never" means "someday." In the meantime, she plays a sprightly instrumental version of "Seasons of Love," and sits down looking suitably pleased with herself.

I am pleased, too, and feeling almost relaxed; things are going very well so far. But now comes Christopher, and he does not look hesitant; he looks positively stricken. This moment, after all, is the final goal of his yearlong effort to learn a simplified version of Mozart's *Turkish Rondo*. (About a month ago we affixed a couple of emphatic A minor chords to the back end and pronounced it done.) He has been playing it, perfectly, every day. Now he sits at the piano, his brow tragically furrowed, and I fear it all may have gone up in smoke.

The only consistent feature of recitals is the element of mystery. With the audience braced for disaster (the brow is really very dramatic), he begins, haltingly, to play. Gradually but unmistakably, the *Turkish Rondo* evolves. The expression on Christopher's face changes to quizzical, as though he is hearing it for the first time and wondering how it will turn out. Near the end he pauses for a particularly long time, and shakes his head slightly; we hold our collective breath. And then whatever has gotten stuck comes unstuck, and Christopher arrives at last at his A-minor chords. As he dashes for his seat, jubilation flickers ever so briefly across his face and disappears.

Matthew is Christopher's age, equally solemn and equally nervous. But his stage fright seems to have an accelerating effect; he races to the piano and is playing before he sits down ... too far to the left, as it turns out, because he is playing two octaves too low. He is clearly perplexed by this—his piece, a Spanish-sounding item called *Night of the Tarantella*, sounds as though the night is very murky indeed—but he can't quite figure out what has gone wrong or how to correct it. So he decides to finish as quickly as possible. Rests are thrown to the winds, quarter notes become sixteenth notes; the night of the tarantella is over in a twinkling, and Matthew exhales, mops his forehead and sits down.

We are nearly halfway through the recital, at a point where I've made an unusual programming choice: this is where I've placed Ellyn, forty-something years old and a close friend of mine, who for the past several months has been taking the first piano lessons of her life. It seemed awkward to position Ellyn according to experience—at the beginning, before little Jenny—or according to age—after the formidable Justin and Haley and Chloe, at the end. So I have decided to put her here, in the middle. She has learned a simple version of "Bye Bye Blackbird" and can play it with such quiet elegance that I don't miss the embellishments of a more advanced player.

I've had a number of adult students, but none has ever been willing to play in a recital before; grown-ups take potential humiliation very seriously indeed. I am impressed by Ellyn's pluck, and happy to have her "Bye Bye Blackbird" on the program. She sits for a moment at the piano with her head bent, her hands in her lap. Then she raises her head and looks at the audience—no, I realize, she is looking at me.

"I can't remember how it starts," she says.

I try not to show my dismay. I remember how it starts, but I am not at all sure I will be able to jump-start her as I did Tara, all those years ago. Adults simply don't have the keen muscle memory and retentive capacity that children have. I walk to the piano and sit next to her. "This is the first chord," I say.

She puts her fingers where mine were. "Okay," she says, "stay there," and she proceeds to play "Bye Bye Blackbird," more quietly even than usual, but perfectly.

Ellyn is one of the most accomplished women I know. She is a best-selling author, a prominent financial writer, an excellent mother and wife; she rows crew and cooks gourmet meals and happens to be beautiful as well. And here she is, able to play her little recital tune only if I am by her side.

Talk about mystery.

She takes a stylish bow, and Damian replaces us on the piano bench. My nerves kick in again, hard. Damian is the hip-hop aficionado who has devoted himself to learning *Für Elise*; for months I have admired his perseverance even while I worried about his lack of progress, as wrong notes continued to wander intractably among the right ones and fresh memory lapses sprouted each week. A month before the recital Damian gave me his most solemn assurance that he could and would master *Für Elise*, and I believed him. Damian's honesty is one of his many charms. Besides, I wanted to believe him: doesn't every recital need at least one *Für Elise?*

But Damian missed his next lesson, and then his next. "He's practicing a lot," his mother assured me when she called with the second cancellation. On the morning of the recital, Damian came for a lesson. "I've been practicing a lot," he said, and then managed to work his halting way through four measures of *Für Elise* before falling silent.

I waited, but no more measures were forthcoming. "Damian," I said very carefully, "you can't play this in the recital tonight."

"No," he agreed sagely.

"When you have been practicing a lot," I went on, trying to keep my voice from rising, "exactly *what* have you been practicing?"

"Well," he allowed, "I've been practicing *In the Hall of the Mountain King* a lot."

"Because *Für Elise* was too hard?"

"Because *Für Elise* is too hard," he echoed, and I could see then that he was embarrassed.

A year or two earlier, Damian had learned a simplified version of the *Mountain King* dance from Grieg's *Peer Gynt* Suite. "Play it for me," I said, and he played it for me with quiet zest and only a couple of mistakes. At the end of his lesson I dashed to my computer, replaced *Für Elise* with *In the Hall of the Mountain King* on page one of the program, printed out the page and drove much too fast to the printer. "Did you print my program yet?" I asked the copy technician, "because if you didn't, we need to replace that page one with this page one." She raised her eyebrows. *"Für Elise* was too hard," I explained.

"Oh," she said, *"Für Elise.* I love that song."

In the Hall of the Mountain King made it into the program, but Damian, as he sits at the piano, looks worried. I am worried too; brilliantly as she weathered it, Ellyn's crisis has reminded me that anything can happen. But Damian proceeds to play his brand-new recital piece beautifully, better than he played it this morning. Yes, there are a few mistakes, but his grave pleasure in this spooky little classic is palpable. His bow afterward is slow and deliberate. He knows he has done well.

There is a long pause before Stephanie arrives at the piano. I remember that there is a recital breakdown in her past; since we inaugurated her "Beatles" phase, though, she has made it through "Sgt. Pepper's Lonely Hearts Club Band" and "Blackbird" without misfortune. For tonight's recital she has learned "Fool on the Hill," and has played it for weeks with a great deal of finesse and one consistent small mistake. I have recently abandoned my attempts to fix this, having discovered the hard way that when a student is forced to correct a longstanding mistake right before a recital, the rest of the piece frequently unravels. And sure enough, she plays her song beautifully; that single mistake is her good-luck charm.

Monica, whose Beatles phase was every bit as intense as Stephanie's, has recently branched out into other kinds of music. Her taste is highly idiosyncratic but always interesting, and she has learned a complicated, mellifluous piece called *Ghost Dance* for the recital. I decide to enjoy myself; I have been impressed by her developing technique and her intense musicality, and I love the way she plays this piece. Tonight she is playing it better than ever. Her fingers are fleet and agile, the phrasing is sensitive and the transitions seamless. In the middle of a phrase, she stops.

She looks over at me as if she just thought of a question she needed to ask. I wait. The audience waits. Finally, I say, "Monica, go back to the beginning of that section and start again." She does. More beautiful playing, more graceful phrasing. She reaches the same place and stops again. I wait. The audience waits. She looks at me again. She seems to remember the question. "Can I just sit down?" she says.

Well, anything can happen, and so it has. I have no way to explain why this particular thing has happened. "Yes, you can sit down," I say. The applause is thunderous, as though she is an injured player leaving the ball field. She looks impressively calm as she heads for her parents at the back of the recital hall. Still, it's painful to see her derailed in the midst of such a fluent performance. I hope she can hear the applause, and that it will make some difference in the way she remembers this.

Being the performer to follow a mishap is never easy. If anyone can pull it off, though, Tanya can. She has been playing the first movement of the *Moonlight* Sonata for an entire year, and she is eager to show it off. I imagine, too, that she doesn't want to be outshone by her brother Damian's successful performance. She is looking glamorous in heels and hoop earrings; her hair is elaborately braided. She's nervous, of course, and as she begins to play her foot is a bit heavy on the pedal. But within a few measures the nervousness is replaced by concentration, and she is absorbed in moving through the dark and beautiful harmonies she has loved for so long. She plays with power and intensity and a kind of innocence, as though no one had ever played this piece in a recital before; I realize that she had made the *Moonlight* Sonata hers, just as surely as Whitman's poem belonged for a moment to me, all those years ago. The audience is clearly moved. Anything can happen, and this has, too.

I would not have guessed that feisty, strong-willed Pia would be rattled by the recital, but she looks uncharacteristically timid as she walks to the piano. She wipes her hands on her skirt and plunges into her beloved Chopin waltz, pumping the pedal, elbows akimbo; she plays it with brio and only a few mistakes, and acknowledges the applause with a sweeping bow. Then she sits back down to perform her original song

"Soñadora." In her light, clear voice she sings rapidly through many verses, accompanying herself with such emphatic chords that her words are mostly unintelligible. It doesn't really matter, though; we are clearly witnessing a very particular and idiosyncratic musical object. And while her willingness to offer this object looks to the audience like confidence, I know what a risk she is taking; it looks to me like courage.

As usual after Pia, Clinton is up next. I have found so far that he invariably plays better in performance than at lessons. I don't take this for granted, though; I know from my own experience that simple self-confidence does not always guarantee a successful performance. I think of my most memorable audition, which was for a master's program at the Boston Conservatory. I went to that audition supremely confident and gave, I thought, an absolutely definitive performance of the Bach C-sharp-Major Prelude—only to look up and find the judges' collective brow pinched and lips pursed. "Excuse me, Ms. Tunstall," said the august chair of the panel, "what happened to the A-sharp-minor passage?"

I could not begin to tell him what had happened to the A-sharp-minor passage. Somehow it had gone AWOL without my even noticing. Even more astonishing, I had managed in something like idiot savant fashion seamlessly to fuse the two sections that came before and after. Such is the power of even subterranean stage fright.

Clinton, however, has told me that he never feels stage

fright of any kind, and I believe him. True to form, he plays "Hallelujah I Love Her So" better than he has ever played it in his life, delivering a truly virtuosic account of that hard-swinging saxophone solo. The audience whoops at the end as if they're in a nightclub. Clinton, taking his succinct bow, is too cool to smile—almost.

As Max walks to the piano, I can practically hear him wishing he had chosen a jazz piece. He has made a vigorous eleventh-hour run at the *Root Beer Rag*, though, and has managed to cram every bit of it into his fingers and brain. Now, energized by competitive ardor, he plays the hell out of it, and earns a few whoops of his own.

The audience feels like whooping, in any case; we are in the home stretch now, and they are clearly enjoying the older students' proficiency. Eddie comes up to play his be-loved Beethoven sonata—not the first movement, which he has not quite been able to master, but the second movement, the one Billy Joel appropriated for his power ballad "This Night." Eddie is clearly as moved by this music as Billy Joel was; Billy may have been inspired to croon lustrously (if un-grammatically) along with the immortal melody line—*This night is mine / It's only you and I*—but Eddie's playing is pow-erful at a much deeper level. That a sixteen-year-old boy is able to communicate such tenderness, such rhapsodic beauty, catches the audience by surprise, though perhaps it shouldn't. I feel sure that while the second movement of the *Pathétique* has been played with more finesse, it has never been played with more earnest and abundant feeling.

Margot comes up looking absolutely bashful—and, in her high-heeled sandals and sleeveless dress, absolutely twenty-five. I have one of the classic recital "moments" with which every piano teacher is familiar, suddenly apprehending the transformation of a student I have known since childhood. I began teaching Margot when she was a little girl; she stopped taking lessons during her early teenage years and then came back last year at the age of seventeen. My internal image of Margot centers around a duet she played with her best friend when they were both twelve. The best friend, also one of my students, was about to move away, and she and Margot wanted to celebrate the eternal nature of their friendship by playing "Over the Rainbow" together in a recital. Which they did, giggling the entire time. After the recital they presented me with a vial of cologne they had concocted by smashing wildflowers. When I uncorked it, it smelled like a stable.

And now here is Margot looking like she's ready for spring break at Virginia Beach. She sits down and works her deliberate way through the crystalline latticework of the arpeggios in Mozart's C-Major Sonata. Afterward, she is still shy but smiling, a little surprised. Her parents, my friends the Deadheads, are probably surprised too. They are certainly delighted.

Debbie is another of my little-girls-turned-teenage-beauties. She is even more reserved than Margot, and she sits at the piano without moving for what seems like a long time. I have the sense that the longer the silence goes on, the harder it is for her to break it; silence has a weight and a resistance that can feel impenetrable. But she has her own quiet reserves of courage, and she manages to begin the Shostakovich piece she has loved and dwelt within for so long. It's a slow piece, and she plays it very slowly; it has a dreamlike quality. Its dark modernist harmonies and severe melodic lines are unfamiliar, almost jarring. But her deep feeling for the music is apparent, and it is a hushed and lovely moment in the recital.

There are three students to go: Justin, Haley and Chloe. While Justin has a slight technical edge, they are all terrific pianists, and so I have decided to order them by age. When Justin comes up to play, the room is very still; at the tender age of thirteen his reputation already precedes him. I am concerned, though, about a factor unknown to most of the audience: some six weeks ago Justin injured his right hand badly in a fencing tournament. He has only recently been able to practice again, and his recital piece, the last movement of the *Moonlight* Sonata, is very difficult even for the healthiest hands, with arpeggios racing up and down the keyboard.

I was eleven, just a couple of years younger than Justin,

when I confronted a similar challenge. A few days before my performance as soloist with the Charleston Youth Symphony in West Virginia, I went down the street to play with friends; it was May, and warm, and we were fooling around on our bikes. For some reason—it escapes me exactly why—I put my left hand on the wheel of a bicycle whose rider began to back up, and the sharp fender sliced into my knuckle. Since the pain was not acute, I didn't panic until I realized I could see layers of exposed muscle and sinew, at which point I leapt on my bike and rode home howling at the top of my lungs. Ten or twelve stitches later, I asked the doctor if he thought I would be able to play in the concert. He shrugged.

My teacher Mrs. Witschey did not shrug. "Of course you'll play," she said. Since moving my index finger might break the stitches, she suggested that I squeeze a tennis ball with my left hand for the next few days, to keep my muscles limber, and continue practicing with my right. I squeezed the ball from morning till night; I was damned if I was going to let all that practicing, not to mention my new lavender dress, go to waste.

I played my concerto with the stitches bulging, which is not as heroic as it sounds; it didn't hurt much, and I made a fair number of mistakes. But it became an entrenched bit of family lore, as such things tend to do. As Justin takes his place on the piano bench, I realize I am watching his own family lore in the making, and I can only hope he has been squeezing his tennis ball.

I needn't have worried, of course. He plays the movement brilliantly, with far fewer mistakes than I made in my Mozart concerto. And he is not simply showing off; he plays with unaffected passion, from the wild bluster of the opening to the transparent sorrow of the second theme. True to his promise, he plays very, very fast. He receives sustained applause, and he deserves it.

But it makes things more difficult for Haley, who has to follow him. Haley suffers fairly acutely from stage fright, and the older she gets, the more she seems to suffer. I can see a trace of panic in her face. This, too, is a recital moment every piano teacher knows: the feeling of being helpless to relieve a student's anxiety. Resorting to superstition, I take a few deep breaths so that she will too. Maybe it works. She begins to play, and she plays splendidly. The Schubert Impromptu cascades from the piano, every note pearl-perfect; is it my imagination or is Haley beginning to relax? On she goes, into the stormy section and out again; she is near the end when she loses her way. Bewildered, she repeats the last few bars and gets entangled again. She looks over at me with something approaching desperation. Even superstition deserts me now, and all I can offer is the same limp suggestion I offered to Monica: "Just start that section again, Haley." So she does, and this time I hold my breath. She makes it through; she recovers her balance and plays beautifully to the end. The applause is once again thunderous, but she looks disconcerted as she takes her seat.

I wish she knew what a triumph she's achieved. I wish she knew how much harder it is to recover from a breakdown than to sail through a performance unscathed. I'll tell her these things, after the recital, but I doubt she'll be able to hear me. Now, though, there is Chloe to attend to—Chloe, my most longstanding student, my graduating senior, who will finish my recital this year. Chloe has spent the last three months refining her interpretation of the Debussy *Arabesque*, polishing every expressive detail, perfecting her technical command of the piece. Chloe has also spent the last three months not memorizing it.

She seats herself at the piano, props her music on the rack and opens it. I station myself at her side, to turn pages. I am not altogether happy, of course, about this state of affairs. But Chloe has helped teach me one of the great lessons every teacher learns: I can control, influence and persuade my students—except when I can't. Chloe will play the *Arabesque* in my recital using the music, or she will not play the Arabesque at all.

And so of course she plays. She unfolds this delicate, powerful music for us with such authority, such a sure sense of its expressive arc, that it's almost as though we can hear the whole piece at once, as one sees a painting whole. There is a moment in the very middle, before the E-major main theme returns, when Debussy veers suddenly into C major, a key that feels and sounds very far from E. He dwells there for a moment; then a single augmented chord takes us, like a magic window, straight back to E major. Chloe plays this brief passage so slowly, so softly, that it becomes the still, haunting heart of the piece. Her audience is rapt.

When she reaches the hushed E octave at the end of the piece she lingers on it, letting the sound die gradually away. Then she puts her hands in her lap, an unexpectedly adult gesture. We share her moment of silence, and finally the applause begins; the audience claps loud and long and happily for her and for all the performers. And then it's over, and my mother is at the refreshments table serving cookies and punch. The parents are relaxed and voluble, the performers wildly relieved. Small children careen around the room dribbling cookie crumbs; smaller ones lie flushed and unconscious on their parents' shoulders; a few students, inevitably, congregate at the piano to play "Heart and Soul." I am told it was a fine recital, and I have to agree; where else, after all, could we have heard "Fool on the Hill" and the *Turkish Rondo*, Debussy and Queen, Ray Charles and Shostakovich and "American Pie," in the space of an hour on a summer evening, free of charge? Parents congratulate one another's children; children give each other giddy high-fives. I manage to find Haley, who is still upset; her mother and I endeavor to make her feel better. In a quiet but compelling aside, her mother tells me that Haley must never again follow Justin on a recital program. Well, yes.

And then, abruptly, they're all gone, leaving me suspended as always between elation and letdown. Every piano recital is a consuming focus of my attention for months. And after it's over, it's just . . . a piano recital. In the great scheme of things, not a monumental event.

But each of my students has passed through a distinct and somehow formative experience. Like every childhood ritual, its importance is not in the great scheme of things but in the fine texture of the developing individual's sense of self. It's enough—it's more than enough—to know that my recital will have its place in the skein of these future adults' gathering childhood memories.

I don't remember ever making a conscious decision that piano recitals would remain a lasting part of my adult life, instead of fading into childhood memory. And yet here I am, in yet another humid June twilight, closing the piano and folding the chairs and turning out the lights. I reflect that it must have something to do with the enduring pull of all my piano teachers—Miss Ortmann, Mrs. Witschey, Mrs. Bane and Mr. Heyne; the redoubtable Madame Dmitrieff, the brilliant Mrs. Gordon. Most of all, perhaps, it has to do with my last piano teacher.

CHAPTER SEVEN

My Last Piano Teacher

*T*he story of my last piano teacher begins with the only period in my life when I did not play the piano. It was during my undergraduate years at Yale, a time when the multiple distractions of academic work, political activism and a beautiful dark-eyed boyfriend led me to abandon the piano entirely for several years. I pursued a major in, of all things, philosophy; I took courses in Russian literature and British labor history and the economics of capital accumulation; I delivered speeches at antiwar demonstrations; I went dancing. I had a wonderful time. I missed playing the piano, sometimes acutely; an essential part of me had gone missing in action. But as my sabbatical from the piano grew longer and longer, I found it harder and harder to contemplate returning. All my technical facility, I was sure, had slipped away, and the thought of missing the octaves in a Brahms intermezzo or fumbling the parallel thirds in a Chopin nocturne was more than I could bear. It was painful to think of violating the music I loved and had once played so well.

I graduated, more or less in spite of myself, and stayed in New Haven for the summer, waiting for my future life to make itself known. Richard Nixon resigned. Turkey invaded Cyprus. Charles Lindbergh died in Hawaii. I, however, continued to drift. And I missed the piano.

It occurred to me that there might be some sort of backdoor way to return. Maybe the prospect of mutilating Brahms was intolerable, but what about trying to play something I never knew how to play before? Jazz came to mind. I had never played jazz in my life. The stakes seemed blessedly low.

Since my boyfriend was taking jazz guitar lessons, I asked him to ask his teacher for the name of someone who taught jazz piano. Which he did, and reported to me that his guitar teacher told him the guy to call was Don Johnston, who had graduated a decade or so earlier and was teaching jazz at a music school in town.

I called the music school and set up an appointment to meet with Mr. Johnston. On a pale Thursday afternoon in late August, I found my way to the school and was directed by the secretary in the front office to Room 201. I was very nervous; jazz suddenly felt like a deep risk after all. To my relief, Room 201 was locked. He had forgotten, or I had gotten the time wrong or he was stuck in traffic. At any rate, I did not have to come up against jazz that day. I decided to look for another way out, so as not to have to walk past the office again, and wandered down the hall to a stairwell. Looking over the railing, I saw a man with curly salt and pepper hair and a thick mustache chaining his bicycle to the railing in the hallway below.

He looked up at me. "Do I have an appointment with you?" he said. I said I thought so. Anxiety locked in again, stronger than before. He took the steps two at a time and produced a key to Room 201.

It was a large room filled with chairs and music stands; two grand pianos stood side by side. Dusty sunlight poured through a high window and made a trapezoid on the floor between the two pianos. Mr. Johnston sat down at one piano and I deduced that I was to sit at the other. "I don't know anything about jazz," I said.

"You don't have to," he said. "Just answer me." He played, briefly, something that sounded to me more like Ravel than jazz. Then he looked over at me. His glasses were thick, but his eyes were blue.

Miss Ortmann had not prepared me for this moment. Nor had Madame Dmitrieff, or Mrs. Witschey or Mrs. Gordon. What he had played had sounded like a question, but I was damned if I knew the answer. I took a breath and played his question back to him as best I could.

He answered immediately, another question, shorter, teasing. I felt slightly faint. I did not know this language. I promised myself never to come back, and then I played something; it sounded feeble and silly to me, but he seemed satisfied. "Now," he said, "just play along with me, play while I play."

"Play what you play?" I said stupidly. "No, not what I play; just anything you feel like playing, while I play." And then he began to play in earnest, some kind of chord progression that was at once rich with sonority and edged with dissonance here and there. I had no idea what the chords were and was reduced to trying notes more or less at random. He seemed to forget I was there. He played louder, softer, faster, slower, at once absorbed and impulsive, as if recounting a dream. And after him I went, nervous, stumbling, heavy-handed, but now and then tripping across a harmonious note or phrase. I don't know how long we played, under the cascade of blond light, but I know that I forgot, from time to time, to feel stupid.

He ended, leaning on a chord until it died away. In an unlooked-for outbreak of nerve, I played a few more notes. He played like a poet, but he grinned like a middle school delinquent. "Cool," he said.

I went the next week, and the next. The lessons evolved

toward something that felt more like jazz. I began to learn about seventh chords, ninth chords; I was introduced to modes. Mr. Johnston decided that the first jazz tune I should work on was "All the Things You Are." After a few weeks I could play a very primitive version, with a chord plunked on every downbeat. He stood behind me, crooning under his breath as I played. *"You are the promised kiss of springtime . . ."* I could not help but notice that I was taking longer and longer each week to decide what to wear to my piano lesson. *"You are the breathless hush of evening . . ."* Mr. Johnston mentioned that I could call him Donald.

I was profoundly relieved to be playing the piano again. And certainly playing jazz badly was easier on my ego than playing classical music badly. But it was not comfortable to be a beginner after so many years of proficiency. My fingers stubbornly refused to remember the intricate voicings of jazz chords; I had to learn them over and over, week after week. When I attempted to improvise, I had trouble playing anything but the major and minor scales I had practiced for so long. I concluded—I was, after all, a beginner—that jazz was hard.

Mr. Johnston—well, Donald—was mostly patient, and always encouraging. He wrote out tunes and chord changes for me to work on; he invented exercises "to loosen up my hands," he said. I didn't know whether he had three students or thirty, but he approached lessons with me as if I were his only pedagogical project. I wanted, intensely, to make his project a success. I spent an hour or two every night in a practice room at the music school, since there was no piano in the communal house where I lived, and I pored over those tunes and exercises. Despite all my years of practicing the piano, I had no idea how to practice jazz. Practicing classical music is a matter of painstaking repetition until you get it exactly right. But with jazz, there are an infinite number of ways to get it right—and to get it wrong. As for those finger exercises, just how loose were my hands supposed to be, anyway? It was maddeningly imprecise, and I left the practice room each night uncertain as to whether anything had happened at all.

At the end of a lesson one week, Donald suggested that I come and hear his trio play at a local club that weekend. I considered the idea of taking my boyfriend, since he was curious about how my lessons were going, but decided against it. Instead, I went with a female friend, a worldly type a few years older than I, who encouraged me to order a whiskey sour.

Had I ever been to a jazz club before? I don't think so. Certainly, I had never had a whiskey sour. The room was small and filled with candlelit smoke; the drink, to my relief, was sweet. I felt like a grown-up. The musicians, although young, were clearly grown-ups, the drummer burly and bearded, the bass player slight and ponytailed. It was a time when Miles Davis and Weather Report and the Mahavishnu Orchestra were inventing electronic jazz, free jazz, fusion jazz and funk jazz, but these guys played what I thought of as real jazz, by turns lyrical and playful, brilliant and bawdy. There seemed to me to be a rueful, ironic smile behind all of its many changes, as though jazz were not only music but a way of knowing. The musicians cocked their heads toward each other, attentive, bemused, like conspirators in on some tremendous secret that was at once delicious and sad. With those broad white hands of his, Donald grabbed great fist-fuls of notes and flung them away, played tight hot synco-pated chords with his left hand and poured cascading runs over them with his right. Broken fragments of melody emerged out of roiling harmonies and then were pulled under again. This was an entirely different relation to the piano than anything I had ever experienced—a sort of free fall, utterly open to hazard, adventure, whim, and at the same time shaped by an organizational instinct and a techni-cal facility I could not even imagine. Was it the whiskey sour? I did not want it to stop. I did not want to stop listen-ing to him, it occurred to me, ever.

But before the set was over, my friend was looking at her watch; her tastes ran to Pink Floyd and the Mothers of In-vention. We paid our tab and left. "That was cool," she said as we walked to her car, "the bass player was cute as hell." I was too busy descending into an abrupt depression to answer. Donald had not even looked my way. Besides, there was the matter of musical hopelessness to contend with. It was obvious that I would never, ever be able to play anything remotely like what I had just heard. So why bother? Why take lessons at all?

At my next lesson I managed to articulate something along these lines. "It just seems, you know, pointless," I said, "pointless to even try."

He considered this. "Well," he said finally, "I guess if the point is to play jazz like me, then it is pointless."

I was surprised. "What other point could there be?"

"To play jazz like you," he said.

"But I don't play jazz," I said.

The grin, then. "We're working on it," he said.

We worked on it. We put a sharp-toothed thirteenth chord on the end of "All the Things You Are" and went on to "Embraceable You." I struggled to understand chord substitutions and to remember the difference between the Dorian and Mixolydian modes. He attempted to teach me a ridiculous stride bass version of "Embraceable You"; it proceeded so slowly the tune was nearly unrecognizable, but Donald pronounced it fabulous. "*Just one look at you / My heart grows tipsy in me,*" he sang, stretching out the words absurdly so I could keep up with him.

I was not aware of my technique improving much, or my confidence for that matter. But with every lesson I grew more certain that I could trust him. No matter how badly I played or how much I faltered, he was never scornful or disparaging. I came to see that as long as I was engaged and stimulated, he was content. And whenever I took a risk, even a small one—that ponderous stride bass for example—he was more than content; he was elated. At the end of every lesson we would revisit the musical conversation we had begun at the very first one, with him at one piano and me at the other. The trapezoid of sunlight on the floor between us trembled and shrank to a sliver as the weeks went by and fall gave way to winter. Sometimes the musical phrases we played at each other were chatty and full of tumbling notes, other times bantering and brief. And sometimes he would play a chord so intricate and sweet that I had no answer. I would look over at him then and find him looking back.

At some point during these weeks I broke up with my boyfriend, who was understandably confused. I told him I needed space. There was not much more I could say; he was a lovely fellow, and this was not his fault. He cried, I cried, I uttered a few more platitudes; and then with considerable courtesy he made a graceful and nonrecriminatory departure from my life.

Then it was Christmastime, and Donald and I made the astounding discovery that my parents and his lived in the same New Jersey town, about a two-hour drive away. He said he was driving home for the holidays with his drummer and the drummer's sister, but there was room in the car for me. Would I like a ride? I would, I said.

They picked me up early the next morning in the drummer's rattletrap little car. Donald was in the passenger seat; the sister, a striking brunette, was in the back seat behind Donald. I climbed in next to her. She spent the next two hours leaning forward and giggling in Donald's ear, her arm draped across his shoulder. I stared out the window, which was stuck slightly open and leaked a thread of icy wind across my face. Why hadn't I figured he had a girlfriend? Of course he had a girlfriend! Of course his drummer's sister was his girlfriend! Why on earth had I allowed myself to believe that our moments of musical intimacy were anything more than clever pedagogy? All the things you are, indeed!

And so forth.

I spent the rest of the day holed up in the pink and lavender bedroom of my high school years, refusing to come downstairs to dinner for all the world as though I were still in high school. The next day was Christmas Eve. Donald called. He and his mother wondered if I would like to come over for lunch.

"How did he find my number?" I gasped to my curious parents after I dried my eyes and put on my cleanest pair of blue jeans. My father allowed as how we were, in fact, in the phone book. My mother brushed my hair out of my eyes and handed me the car keys.

Donald's mother had recently taken a course in Mandarin Chinese cooking, and she had concocted an elegant lunch that went from scallion-flecked soup to cakes soaked in honey. She was a tiny, handsome woman with an easy smile and those Wedgwood-blue eyes. We sat at the kitchen table chasing peanut-oiled snow peas around our plates with chopsticks. Donald seemed suddenly boyish, even shy. But when I left, he asked me to have dinner with him in New York City on the day after Christmas. On the way back to my parents' house I was pulled over for disregarding a stop sign. "Merry Christmas!" I warbled at the police officer as he wrote out the ticket. Two nights later, in a taxi taking us from Lüchow's in the Village to Penn Station, I asked about the drummer's sister.

"Oh, she's just a friend," said Donald. He kissed me, to prove his point. "We can still have piano lessons, right?" he said.

Reader, we still had piano lessons. In the evenings we met for dinner sometimes, or went to the movies; on Saturday nights I drank whiskey sours at a table that came to be thought of, by the waitresses at the club, as mine, and went home to his apartment with him after the last set. He had never gotten around to window shades, and on Sunday mornings I woke out of jazz-soaked dreams dazzled by the pearly winter sunrise and my own happiness. But on Thursdays from three to four o'clock in the afternoon we were teacher and student, pure and simple. It was an hour neither of us wanted to give up.

The lessons were altered, of course, by our growing intimacy. We talked more. We laughed more. We began to develop the repertoire of inside jokes and private silliness that lovers rely on. But we were able somehow to keep the heart of the lesson in place. Donald continued to teach me the art and craft of jazz piano, and I continued—very, very slowly— to learn.

I learned to play "Fly Me to the Moon." I learned to play "Satin Doll." Spring came, full of wind and rain. I struggled with "Cry Me a River." "I'll comp for you, you take a solo," said Donald near the end of a particularly arduous lesson, as if that were any way to relax. I struck out bravely, fumbled, lost my way and stopped. He kept playing. "Silence, that's great," he called over, "inspired choice. Now do something with it." Frustrated, I splashed down on a handful of notes. It sounded worse than I had anticipated. On he played, deadpan. "Perfect," he said, "keep going."

I limped to the end of the solo, but nothing I played sounded right. We both stopped. My head ached. Donald sat for a moment with his eyes closed. Then he opened them and played the first phrase of a Bach invention. I played the second phrase before I remembered what it was. "Aha," he said, "I thought you didn't play that stuff anymore."

"I don't," I said, and that night in the little practice room alone, I tried the invention again and found that it fell from my fingers as though I had been practicing it for a month.

A good teacher knows when a student is ready to take the next step. An extraordinary teacher knows when the next step may be back, toward recovering something lost and crucial. I realized, not for the first time, that Donald was an extraordinary teacher. He had understood that just as beginning to play jazz had helped me through a crisis of confidence about classical music, playing classical music now might help me through an impasse with jazz. And he had understood that he could give me the permission I somehow needed to retrieve my classical identity.

One elegant, long-forgotten contrapuntal phrase; that was all it took. I was surprised at how easy I found it, after all, to slip my old volumes of Beethoven sonatas and Chopin waltzes into the bag with my jazz charts when I went to the practice room at night. I was surprised at how hungry I was for those sonatas, those waltzes, and how much of them, after all, I had retained. My practice sessions went on for hours now, as I hurtled from "Take the 'A' Train" to the *Pathétique* and back again until my ears were ringing and my fingers were sore. I had always loved the feel of sore fingers.

Donald, as it turned out, had a classical identity of his own. Although he had grown up playing jazz, he had managed to acquire a formidable, if accelerated, classical training in college. When he played Chopin, it was inexact but it was thrilling; he stopped just short of swinging the six-teenth notes. He loved to play Bartók, Granados, anything with driving percussive rhythms and thickets of chords. He presented me one day with an arrangement of *The Rite of Spring* for four hands—that is, two pianists at one piano. "Stravinsky arranged it himself," he told me. "He played it with Debussy in Paris." Well, maybe. We began to play it together, and the more we played, the more I had my doubts about that. The arrangement was all crossed hands and tangled arms, fingers flirting with fingers, thigh brush-ing thigh. Did Stravinsky really yearn to entwine with De-bussy? I thought not; I thought this was Stravinsky's gift to lovers.

Lovers, and teachers and students. Donald, I discovered, was not only an extraordinary teacher but an incorrigible one. He could not resist a didactic opportunity or pass up a moment of pedagogical potential. "I think, really, that pas-sage would work better with a different fingering," he would say as we practiced together. "Try putting your thumb under your fourth finger." Or "When you play parallel octaves like that, it really helps to bounce more at the wrist." And some-times, "You're only making mistakes because your shoulders are tense. Relax your shoulders."

"My shoulders have nothing to do with it," I would object at last, when I grew tired of finding that he was right.

"They do, though," he'd respond. Later, of course, alone

in the practice room, I would relax my shoulders, retrieve the lost notes and wonder how he knew.

He knew. He had an uncanny gift for sensing and envisioning the logical next step in a learning process, as well as for glimpsing peculiarly effective solutions to intractable problems. And he loved—let's face it, he was compelled—to share these insights. He taught me new fingering methods, new technical exercises; he taught me new and imaginative ways to practice scales and arpeggios. When the squalls of early spring gave way to layered, fragrant sunshine, we left *The Rite of Spring* on the piano rack and ran to a nearby park, where he taught me to throw a Frisbee so that it curved between the trees. We played through the afternoon—he loved heat, and ran like a jackrabbit—and then collapsed on the grass, where he taught me his favorite yoga poses. Back at his apartment, grass-stained and sweaty, we would make dinner. He knew a thing or two about pasta sauce, which, of course, he taught me.

Naturally, there were times when his tireless pedagogy could be irritating. But mostly, I loved it when he taught me things—because he was never condescending, because his approach was so full of exuberance and high spirits, because his excitement about teaching and learning was so genuine, and so infectious.

And—this was the most important of all—because he loved it when I taught him things. An avid linguist, already fluent in German and decent in Russian, he was delighted when he discovered that I had studied French, and decided that I should begin teaching him immediately. Our French lessons were not as formal as the piano lessons—they took place, usually, over breakfast at a diner near the entrance to the interstate—but they were every bit as purposeful. I would bring an elementary French grammar and a paperback copy of *L'Étranger*, by Camus. *"Je suis, tu es, il est,"* he repeated after me. The corn muffins were about the size of Frisbees, and dripping with butter. *"Nous sommes, vous êtes, ils sommes."*

*"Ils **sont**,"* I corrected him. He loved being corrected. With a couple of verbs under his belt and after several cups of coffee he was, he felt, more than ready for Camus. *"Aujourd'hui, Maman est morte,"* I enunciated slowly.

"Aujourd'hui, Maman est morte," he chanted, his accent perfect. "Today Mother is strong."

" 'Strong' is *forte*," I told him. *"Morte* is 'dead.' "

"Today Mother is dead!" he crowed. After several lessons the pages of *L'Étranger* began to accrue butter stains, jelly stains, which gave Camus's dour story of murder in Algiers a romantic sheen few readers have found there before. Sooner or later, French would remind us of Paris, which would remind us of Debussy and Stravinsky, and back we would go to the piano.

I was working at a part-time job, and Donald taught in the afternoons and played on weekends, so we had time to master

The Rite of Spring. We performed it as part of a spring festival at a local arts center, to a fairly large and enthusiastic crowd. It was my first public performance in years, and I could not have been prouder if I had been playing with Stravinsky.

The success of this performance gave me the confidence to decide to apply to graduate school at several conservatories. As I prepared for auditions, my practice room sessions began of necessity to tilt toward Bach and Beethoven and away from Ellington and Gershwin. Donald was unperturbed. We continued to have lessons on Thursday afternoons, but sometimes after we wheeled through a couple of choruses of "Satin Doll," he would ask me to play one of my audition pieces for him. He knew by then, I think, that I would never be a jazz player, and that my heart lay, after all, in the journey back to classical music.

So I would play for him: a Bach prelude and fugue, or a movement of a Beethoven sonata or a Rachmaninoff prelude. He would have many things to say. Always, I was struck by the sheer range of his perceptions. He would fixate on some tiny detail of fingering or phrasing, parsing and worrying it until he felt I got it exactly right. Then he would move without apparent transition to the most general level of analysis. He would find the precise moment when a Beethoven sonata lifted off from conventional loveliness into something transcendent and mysterious; he would point out the sorrow beneath some silvery modulation in a Bach fugue. And then it would be back to fingerings again. For him there was no disjunction between levels; passionate expression could not succeed without proper fingering. Finally, "Relax your shoulders," he would remind me.

My acceptance by the Manhattan School of Music ended the New Haven chapter of our lives. I moved to New York and went back to school, taking classes in music theory, analysis, ear training, accompanying. Donald went on tour in Europe with his jazz group for several months. I wrote him a letter every day and sent it, more often than not, to someplace he had just left. When he came back from his tour, he proposed; at least, I'm sure he thought he did. "Hey, how soon could we get married?" were, I believe, his exact words.

Six weeks later—on December 26, the anniversary of our first date—we were married in my parents' living room in front of a fiery sunset in the big bay window across from the piano where I had practiced for so many years. I wrote a poem for the occasion and Donald composed a duet for flute and clarinet. "As long as we both shall live," my poem began. In Donald's duet, played by close friends of ours, the flute and clarinet lines danced close to each other, intertwined, angled apart, came together again. Donald's older sister and my two younger ones were bridesmaids in green velvet. My sisters, who loved both Donald and the story of how we met, asked me afterward, "Are you still going to have piano lessons?"

The exact answer, of course, was no. We found an apartment on the Upper West Side; I left the Manhattan School and began graduate studies in musicology at Columbia and got an office job. Donald was consumed with the challenge of making his way as a freelance musician in the city. There was no place in our new lives for a sun-blessed hour of pure pedagogy every Thursday afternoon.

But there was music between us constantly. Donald wrote a series of piano preludes for me, and I learned them, fingerings and all, and performed them. We spent our discretionary income on piano duet music instead of movies, and played through four-hand arrangements of the Beethoven symphonies at breakneck speed: "First one to stop loses," Donald would call out as we careened down a slope of parallel octaves. We went free to Philharmonic rehearsals at Lincoln Center and the second acts of bad Broadway musicals. Walking home, we sang what we could remember of the worst songs.

When I wrote a cycle of poems and Donald set them to music, we discovered that writing together was the deepest, not to mention the most erotic, connection of all. From that time on, and for many years, we wrote together as a matter of course. We wrote songs for musicals, songs for children's videos, songs for jazz albums. We tossed rhymes at each other as we jogged around the Central Park reservoir and whistled ideas for tunes on subways. Traveling in Europe, we always packed manuscript paper. We wrote a comedy song in Heidelberg in the rain; we wrote a tragic ballad on the Italian Riviera. It was an amazing way to be together.

When our first son was born, we wrote a lullaby for him, a simple tune but a good one, we thought. We propped him up in his infant seat and performed it for him—I sang the melody, Donald sang harmony and played piano—and waited anxiously for his reaction as though he were a music critic for the *New York Times*. Fortunately, he liked it. Unfortunately, he liked exactly that rendition of it. If I went to his crib when he cried in the night and crooned the lullaby in his ear, he would cry harder and point insistently in the direction of the music studio. There was no way around it: only when Donald was roused and we stumbled, ragged with sleep deprivation, to the piano and performed the thing complete with harmony, piano accompaniment and all three verses—only then would our tiny musical tyrant be satisfied and consent to go back to sleep. There were nights, I remember, when we performed this forced musicale three or four times. "He's clearly a musical genius," Donald would mutter as we fell back into bed.

Donald still taught private lessons occasionally, although as he pursued a career as a Broadway conductor and arranger, he no longer had time for many students. One evening I came home from my day job at a corporate office and told him I thought I had found him a prospective new student. "He's about forty, he works in the mailroom and his English isn't very good," I said, "but when he found out we're musicians, he told me his dream had always been to take piano lessons. Do you think you'd have time for him?"

"Does he want to learn jazz?" he asked.

"I don't think he cares," I told him. "I think he'd be happy learning to play anything."

"You should teach him," said Donald.

I was taken aback. "What are you talking about?" I said, "I don't know how to teach piano."

"Well, you'd find out," he said, "wouldn't you?"

The next Saturday morning Harry the mailroom clerk came to our apartment and I gave the first piano lesson of my life. Harry was from Haiti. His hands were like knotted planks from his years of handling boxes; his fingers would barely bend, and he could not move them separately at all. I had bought a piano primer for the occasion, but Harry could not get past the first page, a cheery lesson in correct hand position. Every time he tried to apply a finger to a piano key he swiped at least two of them. At the end of half an hour, his forehead beaded with sweat, he handed me a ten-dollar bill and fled. "What should I do?" I asked my former piano teacher.

Even he was nonplussed. "Spend some time talking," he offered finally. "Maybe if he talks he'll relax and his hands will work a little better."

So at the next lesson I asked Harry about his family. He was palpably relieved at not having to watch his hands assault the keys, and eager to tell me about the two little daughters who were the light of his life. "They love music, they just love music," he said.

I had a sudden inspiration. "Harry, listen," I said, "bring your daughters for lessons. You can sit and listen and you'll be learning at the same time."

Harry beamed. He would get three lessons for the price of two, and would learn to play the piano without actually having to play the piano. I beamed back. I had just decided, I realized, to become a piano teacher.

His daughters, eight-year-old Christine and six-year-old Marie, were as adorable as he had said they were. He brought them from Brooklyn every Saturday morning; it took them over an hour on three different subways. I was worried before every lesson, and worried again afterward. They learned nevertheless. Harry, sitting on the sofa and concentrating furiously, clearly felt he was getting his money's worth. By the end of the school year Christine was playing an elegant little piece by Haydn, Marie was expert at "My Hat, It Has Three Corners," and Harry was—well, Harry was proud.

So was Donald. "You're a natural," he said. I didn't know whether or not I was a natural, but I did know that the more I taught these two little girls, the more I remembered long-forgotten lessons with Miss Ortmann and Mrs. Witschey, Madame Dmitrieff and Anita Gordon. My piano teachers, I discovered, were startlingly alive, quite chatty in fact, inside my head.

With the birth of our second son, my fledgling new career was put on temporary hold. Donald and I revived our lullaby for the new baby and were chagrined to find that he was much less interested in our tender harmonies than in the goofy songs his six-year-old brother sang to him. Among his very first words, proclaimed at the top of his lungs, were "all covered with chee-ee-eese." "How about that," said Donald, "another musical genius."

A year after his birth we moved to the suburbs, and there my life as a piano teacher began in earnest. I taught the son of a neighbor, and then the son's friend and then the friend's sister. Gradually, and more or less by chance, I built a practice of lively, interesting, infinitely various young students. Donald, for his part, had found a new teaching venue, working with high school students at a private school in Manhattan on an elaborate yearly cabaret. Even as his career as a theater arranger and conductor continued to grow, he gave those students exactly the same level of energetic commitment he gave to Broadway. And he was endlessly interested in the stories of my own students' ups and downs, celebrating the successes, offering advice about the difficulties. Our conversations would move from a Broadway finale he was arranging to a seven-year-old student of mine who couldn't learn to read bass clef; I never felt that he found one subject less important than the other.

And as our sons grew and began to play, first the drums and then the saxophone and the piano, Donald was delighted by every C chord, every B-flat scale, every thump of the bass drum. Always, of course, he had much to say. Our sons learned, as I had learned before them, that for Donald teaching music was a way—perhaps the most profound way—of expressing love.

....

"NOW IT STILL REMAINS / To be parted by some avid death." I wrote that in the poem I read at our wedding. It is a terrible thing that a marriage between two people as close as we were, for as long as we were, can come apart. But it can, and we did. I did not know, when I wrote the poem, that I would have to endure more than one parting.

After more than twenty-three years of marriage we divorced, amicably, and Donald moved a few blocks away. Less than a year later he developed chronic back pain, which he and his doctors attributed for some time to an ancient back injury. The pain went quickly from chronic to acute. On September 13, 2001, with our horizon still black with smoke from the collapse of the World Trade Center, he was diagnosed with pancreatic cancer. He became rapidly, desperately ill. He fought it tooth and nail. He began work on a new show. He remarried. He bought a Labrador puppy. Less than four months after his diagnosis, he was dead.

The night before he died our sons played for him, on saxophone and piano, an arrangement of a song he and I had written. At his funeral they played another of our songs, called "There's No Forgetting You." If our two boys could conduct themselves with such unimaginable grace and courage, I thought, I should be able to manage my grief.

But I did not know how. I did not know how to comfort them, or to comfort myself; I did not understand how to live in the world without Donald. I was lost.

....

A FEW WEEKS AFTER Donald's death, Jenny comes for a lesson. She is even shyer than usual, a little overwhelmed by the palpable sadness in the house. I can barely remember how to begin. Can you play a G scale, Jenny? I say.

She nods and begins to play the scale very slowly with her right hand. G, A, B . . . a long pause with her tongue caught between her lips, and then her thumb ducks under her third finger and she continues. C, D, E, F—she winces a little—G. She looks at me uncertainly.

"Which note sounds wrong?" I ask her.

She pokes the F. I nod. "Which note should you play instead of F?" Her finger drifts lightly back and forth across the keys and comes to rest silently on the F sharp. "Very good, Jenny," I say. "Now try it again."

She tries it again, and again she plays F instead of F sharp. A third time, faster now and clearly nervous; this time she makes two mistakes, plays E flat and F natural. Her face clenches. "Stupid," she whispers.

For the first time in weeks, I feel like I can breathe. "Jenny," I say, "you're making mistakes because your shoulders are tense. Relax your shoulders."

Surprised, she thinks about that for a minute. Then her shoulders go down. G, A, B, C, D, E . . . F sharp . . . G.

Without quite looking at me, she smiles.

ACKNOWLEDGMENTS

$\mathcal{M}$y inspiration for this book came, first and foremost, from my piano students—the endlessly interesting and varied young people who have sat on my piano bench six days a week for many years. I have learned at least as much from them about the power of music and the life of feeling as they have learned from me about the piano.

Inspiration has come also from the extraordinary piano teachers of my own youth. My memories of their vivid artistry and equally vivid pedagogy make me proud to continue in their tradition.

I am profoundly grateful to have found an agent, my friend Rick Balkin, whose resonant sensibility and clarity of vision helped me to shape and write this book. His spirited support, along with that of his wife, Felice, sustained and encouraged me at every step in the process.

I am equally fortunate to have found in my editor, Bob Bender, a man with the literary equivalent of perfect pitch.

He has seemed to "hear" this book as well as read it, and his combination of gentle guidance and vigorous enthusiasm has been a great gift.

I owe a debt of gratitude to my parents, Peg and Brooke Tunstall, who made sure that my childhood was filled with music and who continue to inspire me with their love of all things beautiful. When I watch them dance together, I understand that music can be visible.

Many thanks go to my friends Ellyn Spragins, Emily Zacharias, Kathleen Friedman, and Sheila Munson for their astute comments and responses at various stages of the writing and editing process.

My sons, Adam and Evan Johnston, grew up thinking it was normal to have a constant stream of people flowing in and out of one's house to play the piano. Extraordinary musicians both, their passionate musical explorations have had an incalculable effect on my teaching; they have widened my horizons, enlivened my understanding and deepened my joy. They teach me daily about music, life and love.